THE
SOUTHERN AIR FRYER
COOKBOOK

THE
SOUTHERN
AIR FRYER
COOKBOOK

75 Comfort Food Classics for the Modern Air Fryer

PAM WATTENBARGER

BRITTANY WATTENBARGER

PHOTOGRAPHY BY EMULSION STUDIO

ROCKRIDGE PRESS

Interior and Cover Designer: Peatra Jariya
Photo Art Director/Art Manager: Karen Williams
Editor: Lauren Ladoceour
Production Editor: Ashley Polikoff
Photography: © 2020 Emulsion Studio

ISBN: Print 978-1-64739-613-8 | eBook 978-1-64739-383-0

R0

To Bryan, my biggest fan,
Ashton, and Critter,
the best granddaughter.

PAM WATTENBARGER

To Justin, Taylor, Alex,
and Dolly Parton.
Thanks for being there.

BRITTANY WATTENBARGER

CONTENTS

~

INTRODUCTION

Our family has deep roots in the South, beginning in 1678 when our ancestors set foot onto the shores of Virginia. They continued across the region, learning new culinary creations wherever they settled. Recipes were passed down, along with the belief that cooking is a family affair—a way to socialize, show love, and be thankful for bountiful gardens and fruit trees.

We're Pam and Brittany Wattenbarger, mother and daughter *and* native Southerners. Pam began cooking as a child, dragging her pint-size dishes into the kitchen with her mom and aunts. She would fill her plates with goodies—tomatoes dripping with juice, thinly sliced cucumbers, or fresh-cut green bell peppers still warm from the sun. Her humble offerings were always served and appreciated with the same gusto as those from the more experienced cooks.

She still loves the Southern food of her childhood—but not the fat and calories. When she discovered the air fryer, it was almost as if she heard the angels sing "hallelujah." She could once again experience the crispy deliciousness that's a hallmark of fried Southern cuisine—using a fraction of the oil of traditional fried cuisine and without the strong odors of fried food filling the house. Country-Fried Rib Chops (page 92) lightly battered on the outside and moist on the inside, Fried Green Tomatoes and Dipping Sauce (page 38), and Fried Okra (page 50) were once again served at her table. Almost anything her Southern soul craved could be made without sacrificing flavor, texture, or tradition.

We were early adopters of the air fryer, excited to find easy ways to create healthier versions of the foods we grew up with. Since we first unwrapped ours one fateful Christmas, we've been adapting Southern classics to fit.

Using an air fryer may sound daunting, but it's really simple. There's no steep learning curve—you'll be turning out delicious, healthier meals in no time. The air fryer can be used to make low-oil versions of just about anything you can imagine, from your favorite appetizers and fried or baked main dishes to creative desserts.

Because we live in the South—the land of heat and humidity—we also love that the air fryer doesn't heat up the house in summer like the oven and stovetop do. Not to mention, air frying is a relatively hands-off process, leaving you plenty of time to get other things done around the house or to finally sit down and have that family meal you've been planning for days.

One of our favorite ways to use the air fryer on weeknights is to make Zucchini-Parmesan Fries (page 55): With just a spritz of oil on the basket and a few minutes of prep, you have a delicious side dish that doesn't bring cries of *Ew!* from anyone in the family. The perennial classic, sweet potatoes, can be tossed with some oil, salt, and pepper, and then air fried until crisp, or mixed with leftover ham cubes and a sweet sauce to create an entire meal. No need to save them for a traditional Thanksgiving spread.

Whether you're new to the air fryer or a verifiable pro, we're sure you'll find new recipes you'll enjoy. Soon, you'll be whipping up fried fish and crispy potatoes for dinner. Let's get started!

CHAPTER ONE

SOUTHERN (AIR) FRIED GOODNESS

Country-style ribs slathered in thick, tangy peach barbecue glaze. Creamy deviled eggs studded with pickles and paprika. Thick, hearty chili. Did you know all these foods can be prepared in the air fryer?

If you love down-home Southern-style cooking, but not all the fat and calories typically associated with it, this versatile appliance will be your new best friend. Whether you're a novice cook or a sesoned pro, we'll walk you through the basics of using the air fryer. Along the way, we'll share some of our favorite classic Southern recipes and creative new twists. Pull up a chair, grab a fork, and let's dig in!

A MODERN TRADITION

Deep-fried food is a Southern tradition. There's nothing like a platter of crisp chicken or fried ham to bring back memories of casual dinners spent with family and friends, our plates and hearts filled to overflowing. Both of us loved childhood meals of fish fries at an aunt's house. The aroma of freshly caught catfish, the snap of potatoes being cut into wedges, and the crackle of hushpuppies as they dropped into the sizzling oil lured everyone into the kitchen for "samples."

Adulthood brought changes to Pam's cooking style. Fried foods were an occasional treat for our family until we discovered the air fryer. After we taste tested our first batch of goodies, there was no turning back. The air fryer found a permanent place in our kitchen.

Brittany used it daily. "Can you bring the air fryer home?" Pam asked, after Brittany "borrowed" her air fryer, again. "I'd like to try a cinnamon roll recipe."

"Sorry, Mom," she said, "I used it so often it broke." That's what you'd call commitment.

We started with fried foods (after all, it is an air "fryer") and began to experiment, discovering some surprising combinations along the way. Try the recipes in this book and we think you will agree: An air fryer is the perfect tool for the modern kitchen, whether you live in the South or not.

EASY TO USE

You know those sweltering summer days when the humidity climbs and it's 110 degrees in the shade? Air fryers solve that problem because they don't heat up the kitchen like a stove. Unlike a deep fryer, there's no huge pot of oil either—saving both money on cooking oil and finding a place to properly dispose of the oil.

Tired of the long preheat times when you turn on the oven? An air fryer can be ready to go in two to three minutes. Best of all, the food cooks faster and more evenly than it does in the stove, oven, or deep fryer, with little hands-on process. It's usually as simple as setting the timer and checking halfway through the cooking process.

For anyone with limited space, the air fryer does double duty. Not only does it fry foods, but many digital models also have one-touch settings to prepare baked goods, cook frozen foods and fresh meats, toast nuts, and heat leftovers.

FLAVOR BOOSTER

Southern classics are known for their golden-brown exterior and insides dripping with juice. Air fryers create this effect by working like small convection ovens. Hot air, filled with tiny oil droplets, circulates evenly around the food. There are fancy scientific words to describe this process. It's called the Maillard reaction, which is a chemical reaction caused when an amino acid and reducing sugar meet in the presence of heat. For our purposes, we will say it results in a crunchy exterior and juicy interior just like Grandma used to make.

HEALTHY COOKING

Pan-frying and deep-frying are the traditional ways of frying foods, and they use a lot of oil—up to 3 cups for a single recipe! Air fryers provide the same flavor, crunch, and mouthfeel using just a fraction of the oil needed for other frying methods—usually 1 to 2 tablespoons. The excess fat drains into the basket beneath the food. Say goodbye to oil-soaked paper towels for draining, films of greasy residue, and purchasing a gallon of oil at a time for cooking.

AIR-FRIED BACON

Bacon is the Southern cook's favorite source of flavor and texture—even when used in moderate amounts. Since so many of the region's recipes include bacon, it's a good idea to air fry up a batch ahead of time and keep it stored in a sealed container in the refrigerator for up to five days. That way, you always have some cooked slices on hand. To do it in the air fryer, cook 8 pieces at a time at 375°F for 5 to 6 minutes. Flip and cook for 5 to 6 minutes more, depending on the degree of crispness desired.

EASY CLEANUP

Tired of washing splattered oil off of walls, the stovetop, and cabinets? With the air fryer, everything is contained. There's no messy grease scattered around the kitchen and no pot of leftover oil left congealing on the stove. Most models have removable parts that are dishwasher safe or can be washed by hand. The outside can be wiped clean with a damp cloth.

THE SKINNY ON AIR FRYERS

Basket fryer? Paddle fryer? Help! There's an overwhelming variety of air fryers available. How do you know which is right for your family? Our no-nonsense guide gives you the skinny—everything you need to know before purchasing this appliance.

Step 1: Consider Size

Air fryers can be purchased in all sizes. Small (1- to 2-quart) sizes are good for individuals, while medium (2.2- to 3-quart) fryers are best for couples. A family of four might need a 5.3- to 5.8-quart version, while larger families—or anyone who cooks in bulk—will likely prefer a 6- to 16-quart fryer. If you choose a small fryer, remember smaller baskets require more work, as they must be shaken during cooking when filled with food and may even require batch cooking.

Step 2: Find Your Style

There are three air fryer styles to choose from—basket-, paddle-, or oven-style air fryers.

- **Basket fryers** cook food inside a basket. Because most baskets must be pulled out and shaken midway through cooking, you'll find a handle on the outside of the basket.

- **Paddle fryers** have a rotating paddle that turns the food to ensure even cooking. They are the most expensive choice and can even make liquid dishes such as risotto.

- **Oven fryers** are more like mini ovens. Not only can they be used to air fry, but they can usually toast, bake, and broil, too.

No matter what type of air fryer you choose or what your skill level might be, you can enjoy our recipes. (For what it's worth, we used a 6-quart basket fryer to create the dishes in this book.) Along the way, we'll dish up tips and sprinkle in some homemade goodness. Soon you'll be singing, "Fry, fry again!"

TODAY'S SOUTHERN KITCHEN

You'll find a few staples in almost any Southern kitchen. We're looking at you, sweet tea and biscuit cutters. With the addition of an air fryer, you'll need a few basic tools and ingredients to help you get the most from your machine. Don't worry. We didn't get wild and crazy. You can find these items at most stores or online.

GOOD SENSE TOOLS

Baking dishes: Your air fryer can be used to prepare everything from cakes and muffins to appetizers and casseroles. To get maximum use from the fryer, you'll want a few dishes. Most oven-safe dishes can be used in the fryer, along with silicone molds, although glass dishes may fracture due to the rapid heating process.

Basting brush: This tool can be used to brush an egg wash over bread, rolls, and pastries, as well as to brush oil on meat during cooking.

Instant-read thermometer: It's easy to accidentally overcook meat in the air fryer. An instant-read thermometer will tell you the internal temperature so you can stop the cooking process immediately, preventing the waste of good food.

Liners: A must for easy cleanup, liners don't have to be expensive. Aluminum foil or parchment paper is all you need.

Oil mister: Use this to lightly coat the inside of the fry basket and take advantage of the air fryer's power to cook with less fat. An oil mister allows you to control the amount of oil used, keep foods from sticking to the basket, and develop a crunchier coating.

Spatula: Choose plastic or nylon to avoid scratching the nonstick surface.

Tongs: These work well in all types of fryers. They can grip chunky or sticky foods and are easier to use in paddle fryers than a spoon. Because metal can scratch the nonstick surface, choose tongs with nylon heads.

FOR THE LARDER

Basic breading: This can be used on meats, vegetables, and fish. To use in the air fryer, roll the ingredients in the breading, dip them into buttermilk or eggs, and roll them in the breading once more.

Buttermilk: No Southern kitchen is complete without a carton of buttermilk. It can be used to tenderize meat, whip up light, fluffy biscuits and pancakes, and create mouth-watering desserts. Buttermilk can be frozen so it's always on hand. Pour buttermilk into ice cube trays and freeze until solid. Remove the cubes from the trays and place them in an airtight, freezer-safe container. Frozen buttermilk should be used within 3 months.

Cooking oil: Lean toward using just a little oil to improve flavor and quality.

Eggs: One of the most versatile ingredients, eggs can be used in egg washes to brown pastry, in baking to help emulsify batter, and as the perennial Southern classic—deviled eggs.

Panko bread crumbs: These add a crispier texture to foods than traditional bread crumbs. They work well on meat, fish, and vegetable dishes to add crunch and flavor.

Spices: A well-stocked spice cabinet can give meals zing. There's no need for expensive spices, like saffron or juniper berries, to make these recipes. Stock the basics (black pepper, cayenne pepper, chili powder, cinnamon, dried oregano, dried thyme, garlic powder, onion powder, paprika, red pepper flakes, and salt) and you'll have almost every spice you need to prepare most of our recipes.

A SPRITZ OF OIL WILL DO YA

Who needs oil when you have an air fryer? Contrary to this common misconception, in reality, lower-fat foods will dry out when cooked at high temperatures. A spritz or brush of oil—usually about 1 to 2 tablespoons—added before or during the cooking process will keep your dishes moist and your family happy.

Because of the high temperatures used during air fryer cooking, knowing an oil's smoking point (or the temperature at which it starts to burn) is important. Here's a list of our favorite oils and their smoking points.

- Avocado oil has a smoke point of 520°F and has a neutral, buttery taste. With its high smoke point, it's perfect for keeping fried foods moist and flavorful.

- Canola oil has a smoke point of 400°F and a light flavor that pairs well with any food.

- Olive oil has a smoke point between 390°F and 468°F; it pairs well with meats, fish, and vegetables.

- Peanut oil has a smoke point of 450°F and is used as the frying oil of choice in many restaurants.

AIR FRYING WISDOM

Is this chicken supposed to be dry? Why do these onion rings look like this? Why is the batter falling off my pickles? These are common questions for cooks new to air fryers. But even if you've used an air fryer before, it's always good to have a quick refresher on how to use it. If you haven't used an air fryer, these tips can save you time and frustration. We learned the hard way, but you don't have to.

SETUP

It's tempting to toss some food in the oven and press a few buttons, but reading the owner's manual provides valuable information on cooking times and extra features—some you might not discover on your own.

Place the air fryer on a level, heat-resistant surface, making sure to allow space on all sides of the appliance for air to circulate. Aim for around five inches on all sides, behind, and above. Never place the fryer on top of the stove or in the oven, as the heat will damage the fryer and the cord.

Wash all removable parts before first use and check for any misplaced cardboard stuck inside the air fryer. Some models suggest a test run before the first use. If so, follow the manufacturer's directions in the instruction booklet.

COOKING

No one wants to eat a piece of food that's soggy, limp, or unevenly cooked. Fortunately, most of these problems can be avoided with a little prep work and a few kitchen secrets.

◆ Before adding meat or veggies to the fryer, cut them into small, uniform pieces.

◆ Preheating the air fryer before use will help ensure even cooking and speed up the cooking process. *Most of the time.* Packaged, prepared frozen convenience foods won't require preheating.

◆ When filling the basket, don't overcrowd it. Most baskets are small, and it's tempting to cram them full of food to prepare meals more quickly, but it's better to cook in small batches.

◆ If items like French fries are stacked in the basket, you'll need to shake the basket midway through the cooking cycle. Carefully remove the basket from the fryer, gently shake the basket up and down, and replace the basket in the fryer.

♦ Avoid pouring oil or liquid into the fryer basket, as it could cause a fire. For added safety, don't place items on top of the fryer, including that cooking mitt you can never seem to find when you need it. The inside of the oven can reach several hundred degrees in a matter of minutes, and the outer surface may become hot during use. Use caution when opening or touching the appliance.

CLEANUP

Cleaning the air fryer can be done in minutes. When you have finished cooking, unplug the air fryer and allow it to cool. Any removable parts (the basket, pan, and tray) can be placed in the dishwasher or washed by hand in warm, soapy water. If food has stuck to the tray or basket, allow it to soak in warm water to loosen the particles before washing as usual. Most air fryer baskets, pans, and trays are covered with a nonstick surface. To prevent damage to the surface, never use an abrasive cleaner or sponge. Be sure the removable parts are completely dry before returning them to the fryer.

The inside and outside of the air fryer can be cleaned by wiping it with a soft cloth dipped in hot water. If any food is stuck to the top of the air fryer, use a soft-bristle brush or toothbrush and hot water to remove the particles. Clean the air fryer after each use and allow it to cool down for 30 minutes before putting it away.

WHEN THINGS GO CATAWAMPUS

Sometimes things don't go as planned when we use the air fryer. Finished dishes are dry, soggy, or chewy. Sometimes the air fryer doesn't work. When that happens, we've noticed it never hurts to see if someone forgot to plug it into the outlet or check the circuit breaker. We've found four things that might go catawampus with the air fryer and suggest what you should do if any of them happen.

LACK OF CRISPNESS

Air fryers need a small amount of oil to cook food properly. If you notice your food is not browning or becoming crisp, you may not have added enough oil. Add an extra teaspoon of oil, make sure you haven't overcrowded the basket, and flip food repeatedly throughout the cooking process. You can also lightly coat the food with oil before placing it in the fryer.

ODD AROMAS

This is the easiest fix! Your air fryer probably needs a thorough cleaning. Follow our cleaning instructions found on page 9. The best way to prevent this again is to clean the fryer after every use.

BLACK SMOKE

If you notice black smoke coming from the surface, turn off the air fryer and immediately unplug the machine. Call the manufacturer to determine which steps to take next.

WHITE SMOKE

While scary, this usually means you are cooking food with a high fat content or using too much oil. Stop cooking and pat the food to remove excess oil, then cook as directed. Clean the oil pan to remove excess oil.

SUREFIRE TIPS

Ready to impress your friends and family with your air fryer skills? These dos and don'ts will help you receive compliments and bring home empty plates.

1. **Convert the recipe from oven to air fryer.** You can do this by lowering the temperature 25 degrees and reducing the traditional cooking time by 20 percent. For example, if a dish cooks in a 350°F oven for 30 minutes, reduce the heat to 325°F and cook for 24 minutes in the air fryer.

2. **Convert the recipes for special diets.** Recipes can be made gluten-free, egg-free, or vegetarian by replacing ingredients as needed. Replace the flour used in a recipe with a one-to-one measure of gluten-free baking flour. Replace eggs with your favorite egg-free substitute, and replace meats with tofu or veggie crumbles. Be aware that changing the recipe can affect the taste, texture, and cooking time of a finished dish.

3. **Use a liner.** This helps prevent food from slipping through the cracks in the tray and creating a burned mess in the bottom of the air fryer basket.

4. **Pat food dry before placing it in the basket.** Extra moisture left on food may cause it to steam when cooking rather than fry.

5. **Don't use a nonstick cooking spray in the air fryer.** These have additives that could damage the nonstick coatings of the basket and tray. A better choice to keep food from sticking is to spritz the tray with a light vegetable oil spray or olive oil.

6. **Don't use heavy batters.** Wet batter tends to fall off food. When making things like corndogs, onion rings, or fried pickles, you'll need a thicker flour-based batter. The rule of thumb is a three-part dipping process: Dip the ingredients in flour, then into an egg coating, and finish by re-dipping into the flour mixture or dipping into bread crumbs.

AIR FRYIN' UP A STORM

Brittany learned to cook in an unconventional way. When she was 10 years old, she and her best friend, Taylor, raided Pam's spice cabinet to create such concoctions as Spaghetti Exotica, a blend of noodles with 10 different spices, most of which didn't go well together. Pam often found them in her kitchen—after raiding a bush in the yard—trying to discover if the ingredients they had chosen for their latest meal were poisonous. Brittany's an excellent cook now and can toss together seemingly unrelated concoctions to make an appetizing meal.

Half the fun of using an air fryer is experimenting with different foods and flavor profiles. Pam and Brittany still experiment with various spices, although now Brittany experiments with combinations that *complement* each other.

After you've tried the recipes in the book, turn to the back. We've included charts for your own creative mixing and matching. Here's where you'll find cooking times for your favorite fresh and frozen ingredients, plus suggestions for combining them with the various spice mixes and breading mixtures found throughout the book.

But, don't just take our suggestions! Get creative and find your own favorite combinations. Mix and match the suggestions on the charts. Swap out Creole Seasoning (page 16) in the Fried Green Tomatoes and Dipping Sauce (page 38) for Italian-Style Seasoning (page 17). Use ham instead of bacon in the Green Beans with Bacon (page 56). Substitute a spice variation with your own version. Maybe you have your own favorite secret family recipe for dredging. Who knows? You might create your own Spaghetti Exotica.

ABOUT THE RECIPES

The recipes in this book cover everything from classics, like Fried Catfish with Dijon Sauce (page 68) and fluffy Hushpuppies (page 44), to some surprising new things that aren't normally fried, like Deviled Eggs (page 43) or Pecan Rolls (page 29). We've included basic spice mixes and dips in chapter 2 that you can use over and over again in the recipes that follow. Plus, we've added recipe labels to help with meal planning. You'll find at least one of these labels on every recipe in the book:

Family Favorite: These recipes will serve at least four people and feature kid-friendly ingredients.

New Tradition: These recipes include tweaks on a traditional dish to adjust for modern tastes.

True Classic: A traditional Southern recipe that doesn't include any adjustments to the original flavor or ingredients.

We tested our recipes in a basket-style, Instant Pot brand Vortex 6-quart air fryer. This appliance usually prepares about 4 to 6 servings. Depending on the size and brand of your air fryer, the temperatures used in our recipes might need to be adjusted up or down, and there might be slight differences in serving sizes.

Some recipes—like our Classic Fried Chicken (page 78)—have been carefully guarded family recipes through several generations. Others are newer editions of classics refined and "crafted with love," as Pam's children would say. A few were thrown together on days we were tired, hungry, and wanted dinner in a hurry. No matter where you are on your cooking journey, we hope these recipes will help you create fond memories over family dinners. And, if the air fryer helps make cooking easier and requires less cleanup, that will be our little secret.

CHAPTER TWO

TRIED AND TRUE MIXES

CREOLE SEASONING

TRUE CLASSIC

Makes: ½ cup · **Prep:** 10 minutes

Did you know Cajun- and Creole-style seasonings are different? Cajun seasoning is associated with the Acadians, French colonists who migrated from Canada in the early 1800s, and is traditionally used in more rural parts of Louisiana, whereas Creole cooking is often featured in New Orleans. Both seasonings are used interchangeably for breading and can be used as dry rubs.

---

4 teaspoons salt

4 teaspoons garlic powder

5 teaspoons paprika

2 teaspoons freshly ground black pepper

2 teaspoons onion powder

2 teaspoons cayenne pepper

2 teaspoons dried oregano

2½ teaspoons dried thyme

1 teaspoon red pepper flakes

1. In a small bowl, whisk the salt, garlic powder, paprika, black pepper, onion powder, cayenne, oregano, thyme, and red pepper flakes until blended.
2. Store the mixture in an airtight container in a cool, dark place. The seasoning blend should retain its flavor for 1 year if fresh spices are used to make it.

◆ **Cajun Seasoning:** Omit the 2 teaspoons oregano and 1 teaspoon of black pepper from Creole Seasoning. Add 1 teaspoon white pepper and 1 teaspoon ground cumin.

◆ **Tex-Mex Seasoning:** Mix 3 tablespoons chili powder, 2 tablespoons ground cumin, 1 tablespoon black pepper, 1 tablespoon salt, 1 tablespoon garlic powder, and 1½ teaspoons red pepper flakes until blended.

Per Serving (1 teaspoon): Calories: 5; Total fat: 0g; Saturated fat: 0g; Cholesterol: 0mg; Sodium: 389mg; Carbohydrates: 1g; Fiber: 0.5g; Protein: 0g

BLACKENED SEASONING

TRUE CLASSIC

Makes: ½ cup · **Prep:** 10 minutes

Use fresh spices to make this delicious seasoning that's good on chicken, steaks, fish, and vegetables. Want your expensive spices to stay fresh longer? Keep them tightly sealed, out of direct sunlight, and away from heat and moisture.

2 tablespoons paprika

4 teaspoons salt

1 tablespoon freshly ground black pepper

2 teaspoons onion powder

2 teaspoons garlic powder

2 teaspoons dried thyme

2 teaspoons dried oregano

2 teaspoons cayenne pepper

1 teaspoon dried cumin

1 teaspoon dry mustard

1 teaspoon celery seed

1. In a medium bowl, whisk the paprika, salt, black pepper, onion powder, garlic powder, thyme, oregano, cayenne, cumin, dry mustard, and celery seed until blended.
2. Store in an airtight container in a cool, dark place. The seasoning blend should retain its flavor for 1 year if fresh spices are used to make it.

◆ **Chili Seasoning:** Mix 2 tablespoons ground chiles, 4 teaspoons salt, 2 teaspoons ground cumin, 2 teaspoons red pepper flakes, 2 teaspoons garlic powder, and 2 teaspoons sugar until blended.

◆ **Italian-Style Seasoning:** Mix 2 tablespoons dried basil, 2 tablespoons dried oregano, 2 tablespoons dried rosemary, 2 tablespoons dried marjoram, 2 tablespoons dried cilantro, 2 tablespoons dried thyme, and 2 tablespoons dried savory until blended.

Per Serving (1 teaspoon): Calories: 5; Total fat: 0g; Saturated fat: 0g; Cholesterol: 0mg; Sodium: 389mg; Carbohydrates: 1g; Fiber: 0.5g; Protein: 0g

ALL-PURPOSE BREADING

FAMILY FAVORITE

Makes: 2¼ cups · **Prep:** 10 minutes

Coat everything from meat to vegetables with this breading. To get the crispy texture Southerners love, coat the foods with the seasoned flour, dip them into a beaten egg, and recoat with the flour mixture or roll in panko bread crumbs. Lightly spritz the food on all sides with oil after placing it in the air fryer.

2 cups all-purpose flour

1 teaspoon salt

1 teaspoon garlic powder

1 teaspoon dried parsley

1 teaspoon freshly ground black pepper

1 teaspoon paprika

In a medium bowl, whisk the flour, salt, garlic powder, parsley, pepper, and paprika until combined. Refrigerate the mixture in an airtight container for up to 1 year.

♦ **Nashville Hot Breading:** Add 2 tablespoons light brown sugar and 1 teaspoon chili powder to the All-Purpose Breading. Omit the black pepper and replace it with 1 teaspoon cayenne.

♦ **Salt-Free Breading:** Mix 3 cups all-purpose flour, 2 tablespoons dried parsley, 2 tablespoons garlic powder, 2 teaspoons dill weed, 2 teaspoons onion powder, 2 teaspoons dried chives, 1 teaspoon black pepper, 1 teaspoon dried oregano, and 1 teaspoon onion flakes until blended.

♦ **Bread Crumb Coating:** Mix 1 cup Italian-seasoned bread crumbs, 1 teaspoon dried basil, 1 teaspoon dried oregano, 1 teaspoon dried parsley, and ½ cup grated Parmesan cheese until blended. Just before using, stir in ¼ cup beef broth.

Per Serving (¼ cup): Calories: 103; Total fat: 0.5g; Saturated fat: 0g; Cholesterol: 0mg; Sodium: 260mg; Carbohydrates: 22g; Fiber: 1g; Protein: 3g

HOT HONEY MUSTARD DIP

TRUE CLASSIC

Makes: 1⅓ cups · **Prep:** 3 hours 10 minutes

Spicy foods are hit or miss in our family. The kids love them, but Pam's husband, Bryan, not so much. When they were dating, Pam offered him a small bite of jalapeño. Instead, he ate the entire thing in one bite and promptly washed it down with three glasses of soda. This recipe, though, he approves.

¾ cup mayonnaise
⅓ cup spicy brown mustard

¼ cup honey
½ teaspoon cayenne pepper

1. In a medium bowl, stir together the mayonnaise, mustard, and honey until blended.
2. Stir in the cayenne. Cover and chill for 3 hours so the flavors blend.
3. Keep refrigerated in an airtight container for up to 3 weeks.

♦ **Spicy Garlic Honey Mustard Dip:** Mix ½ cup Dijon mustard, 1 tablespoon apple cider vinegar, 1 tablespoon honey, 2 teaspoons minced garlic, 2 teaspoons freshly squeezed lemon juice, ¼ teaspoon red pepper flakes, and ¼ teaspoon cayenne pepper until blended. Refrigerate for 3 hours to meld the flavors.

♦ **Honey Mustard Glaze:** Mix 1 cup light brown sugar, ½ cup pineapple tidbits with juice, ¼ cup drained, chopped maraschino cherries, ¼ cup cornstarch, and 1 tablespoon Dijon mustard until blended. Spoon over pork, chicken, or fish before cooking.

♦ **Honey Mustard Vinaigrette:** Whisk 1 cup vegetable oil, ½ cup distilled white vinegar, 3 tablespoons honey, 1½ tablespoons Dijon mustard, 2 teaspoons salt, 1 teaspoon pepper, ½ teaspoon hot sauce, and 1 teaspoon garlic powder until combined. Refrigerate for 2 to 3 hours to meld the flavors.

Per Serving (1 tablespoon): Calories: 70; Total fat: 6g; Saturated fat: 1g; Cholesterol: 3mg; Sodium: 100mg; Carbohydrates: 3g; Fiber: 0g; Protein: 0g

PEACHY BARBECUE SAUCE

NEW TRADITION

Makes: 2¼ cups · **Prep:** 10 minutes

Every Southern state has its own version of barbecue sauce. In North Carolina, it's a tangy, vinegar-based one. Alabama boasts a mayonnaise-based white sauce. Louisiana is known for its touch of Cajun heat. Although the traditional sauce in Georgia is thick and sweet, we've added a true Georgia classic—peaches—to create an entirely new flavor profile.

1 cup peach preserves
1 cup ketchup
2 tablespoons apple cider vinegar
2 tablespoons light brown sugar

1 teaspoon chili powder
½ teaspoon freshly ground black pepper
½ teaspoon dry mustard

1. In a medium bowl, stir together the peach preserves, ketchup, and vinegar until blended.
2. In a small bowl, whisk the brown sugar, chili powder, pepper, and dry mustard to combine. Add the brown sugar mixture to the peach preserves mixture. Mix well to combine.
3. Transfer the barbecue sauce to an airtight container. Refrigerate for up to 1 week until ready to use as a sauce or marinade.

◆ **Apricot Barbecue Sauce:** Omit the peach preserves. Use 1 cup apricot jam instead. This works well with chicken dishes.

◆ **Cherry Barbecue Sauce:** Omit the peach preserves. Use 1 cup cherry preserves instead. This pairs well with pork and chicken.

◆ **Orange Barbecue Sauce:** Omit the peach preserves. Use 1 cup orange preserves to dress up various cuts of pork.

Per Serving (¼ cup): Calories: 138; Total fat: 0g; Saturated fat: 0g; Cholesterol: 0mg; Sodium: 285mg; Carbohydrates: 35g; Fiber: 0g; Protein: 0g

PECAN TARTAR SAUCE

NEW TRADITION

Makes: 1¼ cups · **Prep:** 1 hour 20 minutes

The pecan, the famous Georgia nut, is the only major nut tree native to North America. The name comes from an Algonquin word meaning "all nuts that require a stone to crack." The United States produces more than 90 percent of the world's pecan supply. Toasted pecans add a satisfying crunch to this tartar sauce.

4 tablespoons pecans, finely chopped

½ cup sour cream

½ cup mayonnaise

½ teaspoon grated lemon zest

1½ tablespoons freshly squeezed lemon juice

2½ tablespoons chopped fresh parsley

1 teaspoon paprika

2 tablespoons chopped dill pickle

1. Preheat the air fryer to 325°F. Spread the pecans in a single layer on a parchment sheet lightly spritzed with oil. Place the pecans in the air fryer. Cook for 7 to 10 minutes, stirring every 2 minutes. Let cool.
2. In a medium bowl, mix the sour cream, mayonnaise, lemon zest, and lemon juice until blended.
3. Stir in the parsley paprika, dill pickle, and pecans. Cover and refrigerate to chill for at least 1 hour to blend the flavors. This sauce should be used within 2 weeks.

♦ **Walnut Tartar Sauce:** Substitute 4 tablespoons chopped toasted walnuts for the pecans.

♦ **Sweet Tartar Sauce:** Omit the toasted pecans and add 1 teaspoon sugar.

♦ **Fast Tartar Sauce:** Mix 1 cup mayonnaise, 1 tablespoon pickle relish, 1 teaspoon minced onion, ½ teaspoon salt, and ½ teaspoon black pepper. Refrigerate to chill for 1 hour to meld the flavors.

Per Serving (1 tablespoon): Calories: 60; Total fat: 6g; Saturated fat: 1.5g; Cholesterol: 6mg; Sodium: 46mg; Carbohydrates: 1g; Fiber: 0g; Protein: 0g

CHAPTER THREE

DOWN-HOME BREAKFAST

DROP BISCUITS

TRUE CLASSIC

Serves: 5 · **Prep:** 10 minutes · **Fry time:** 9 to 10 minutes

These biscuits (pictured on page 22) are delicious with honey butter. To make your own, mix ¾ cup salted butter, at room temperature, and ¼ cup honey until blended. Experiment with different flavors of honey, like tupelo, wildflower, orange blossom, or blackberry for completely new tastes.

4 cups all-purpose flour

1 tablespoon baking powder

1 tablespoon sugar (optional)

1 teaspoon salt

6 tablespoons butter, plus more for brushing on the biscuits (optional)

¾ cup buttermilk

1 to 2 tablespoons oil

1. In a large bowl, whisk the flour, baking powder, sugar (if using), and salt until blended.
2. Add the butter. Using a pastry cutter or 2 forks, work the dough until pea-size balls of the butter-flour mixture appear. Stir in the buttermilk until the mixture is sticky.
3. Preheat the air fryer to 330°F. Line the air fryer tray with parchment paper and spritz it with oil.
4. Drop the dough by the tablespoonful onto the prepared tray, leaving 1 inch between each, to form 10 biscuits.
5. Bake for 5 minutes. Flip the biscuits and cook for 4 minutes more for a light brown top, or 5 minutes more for a darker biscuit. Brush the tops with melted butter, if desired.

◆ **Spice It Up:** Add 1 teaspoon of Cajun Seasoning (page 16) to the dry ingredients before making the biscuits.

◆ **Garlic-Cheddar Drop Biscuits:** Add 1 teaspoon minced garlic and ½ cup shredded Cheddar cheese before adding the buttermilk.

Per Serving (2 biscuits): Calories: 530; Total fat: 18g; Saturated fat: 9.5g; Cholesterol: 40mg; Sodium: 507mg; Carbohydrates: 78g; Fiber: 2.5g; Protein: 12g

BOURBON FRENCH TOAST

NEW TRADITION

Serves: 4 · **Prep:** 15 minutes · **Fry time:** 12 minutes

We discovered quality bourbon at a tasting during a Kentucky distillery tour. When asked if we could taste the caramel notes, we said yes. It turns out we were wrong and were classified as those people with whom connoisseurs would only share their cheap bourbon. Since then, we've expanded our tastes. Use pecan bourbon to give this recipe oomph.

2 large eggs

⅔ cup milk, whole or 2%

1 tablespoon butter, melted

1 teaspoon vanilla extract

2 tablespoons bourbon

8 (1-inch-thick) French bread slices

1 to 2 tablespoons oil

1. In a shallow bowl, whisk the eggs with 2 tablespoons water until blended. Whisk in the milk, melted butter, vanilla, and bourbon.
2. Preheat the air fryer to 320°F. Place a piece of parchment paper in the air fryer and spritz it with oil.
3. Dip both sides of 4 bread slices into the batter. Place the slices on the prepared parchment. Cook for 3 minutes. Flip the bread and cook for 3 minutes more. Repeat with the remaining 4 bread slices.

◆ **Moonshine French Toast:** Omit the bourbon. Use 2 tablespoons of your favorite flavored moonshine to give this a new twist. Some good flavors to try are apple pie, maple bacon, and butter pecan.

Per Serving: Calories: 368; Total fat: 12g; Saturated fat: 4g; Cholesterol: 105mg; Sodium: 565mg; Carbohydrates: 46g; Fiber: 2g; Protein: 14g

MISSISSIPPI SPICE MUFFINS

TRUE CLASSIC

Makes: 12 muffins • **Prep:** 15 minutes • **Fry time:** 13 minutes

The muffins' darker color reminds people of the mighty (muddy) Mississippi River. For uniform size, use an ice cream scoop to fill the muffin cups half full.

4 cups all-purpose flour

1 tablespoon ground cinnamon

2 teaspoons baking soda

2 teaspoons allspice

1 teaspoon ground cloves

1 teaspoon salt

1 cup (2 sticks) butter, room temperature

2 cups sugar

2 large eggs, lightly beaten

2 cups unsweetened applesauce

¼ cup chopped pecans

1 to 2 tablespoons oil

1. In a large bowl, whisk the flour, cinnamon, baking soda, allspice, cloves, and salt until blended.
2. In another large bowl, combine the butter and sugar. Using an electric mixer, beat the mixture for 2 to 3 minutes until light and fluffy. Add the beaten eggs and stir until blended.
3. Add the flour mixture and applesauce, alternating between the two and blending after each addition. Stir in the pecans.
4. Preheat the air fryer to 325°F. Spritz 12 silicone muffin cups with oil.
5. Pour the batter into the prepared muffin cups, filling each halfway. Place the muffins on the air fryer tray.
6. Air fry for 6 minutes. Shake the basket and air fry for 7 minutes more. The muffins are done when a toothpick inserted into the middle comes out clean.

♦ **Brown Sugar Spice Muffins:** Place ½ cup packed light brown sugar into a shallow dish. Brush the tops of the cooked muffins with 1 tablespoon melted butter and dip the muffin tops into the brown sugar.

Per Serving (1 muffin): Calories: 474; Total fat: 19g; Saturated fat: 10g; Cholesterol: 71mg; Sodium: 210mg; Carbohydrates: 71g; Fiber: 2g; Protein: 6g

JOHNNY CAKES

TRUE CLASSIC

Serves: 4 · **Prep:** 10 minutes · **Fry time:** 10 to 12 minutes

When mixing batter for muffins, biscuits, pancakes, or these johnny cakes, use a whisk instead of a spoon. It's ideal for precisely blending ingredients so you're less likely to overmix.

½ cup all-purpose flour

1½ cups yellow cornmeal

2 tablespoons sugar

1 teaspoon baking powder

1 teaspoon salt

1 cup milk, whole or 2%

1 tablespoon butter, melted

1 large egg, lightly beaten

1 to 2 tablespoons oil

1. In a large bowl, whisk the flour, cornmeal, sugar, baking powder, and salt until blended. Whisk in the milk, melted butter, and egg until the mixture is sticky but still lumpy.
2. Preheat the air fryer to 350°F. Line the air fryer tray with parchment paper.
3. For each cake, drop 1 heaping tablespoon of batter onto the parchment paper. The fryer should hold 4 cakes.
4. Spritz the cakes with oil and cook for 3 minutes. Turn the cakes, spritz with oil again, and cook for 2 to 3 minutes more. Repeat with a second batch of cakes.

♦ **Southern Know-How:** Baking powder is an essential ingredient in the kitchen, but it won't last forever. It should be replaced about once a year. To test for freshness, mix a small amount of baking powder with warm water. If it bubbles, it is fresh.

Per Serving (2 cakes): Calories: 409; Total fat: 11g; Saturated fat: 4g; Cholesterol: 60mg; Sodium: 630mg; Carbohydrates: 68g; Fiber: 2.5g; Protein: 9g

TWO-CHEESE GRITS

NEW TRADITION

Serves: 4 • **Prep:** 10 minutes • **Fry time:** 10 to 12 minutes

The new tradition here is cream cheese, and the easiest way to soften it is to remove it from its foil wrapper and place it on a microwave-safe plate. Microwave 3 ounces on high power for 10 to 15 seconds, or 8 ounces for 15 to 20 seconds.

⅔ cup instant grits

1 teaspoon salt

1 teaspoon freshly ground black pepper

¾ cup milk, whole or 2%

1 large egg, beaten

3 ounces cream cheese, at room temperature

1 tablespoon butter, melted

1 cup shredded mild Cheddar cheese

1 to 2 tablespoons oil

1. In a large bowl, combine the grits, salt, and pepper. Stir in the milk, egg, cream cheese, and butter until blended. Stir in the Cheddar cheese.
2. Preheat the air fryer to 400°F. Spritz a 6-inch air fryer–safe pan with oil.
3. Pour the grits mixture into the prepared pan and place it on the air fryer tray.
4. Cook for 5 minutes. Stir the mixture and cook for 5 minutes more for soupy grits or 7 minutes more for firmer grits.

◆ **Spice It Up:** Omit the Cheddar cheese. Add 1 tablespoon chopped jalapeño pepper and 1 cup shredded pepper Jack cheese to the mixture.

Per Serving: Calories: 354; Total fat: 26g; Saturated fat: 13g; Cholesterol: 108mg; Sodium: 1,079mg; Carbohydrates: 19g; Fiber: 1g; Protein: 12g

PECAN ROLLS

FAMILY FAVORITE

Makes: 12 rolls · **Prep:** 20 minutes · **Fry time:** 20 to 24 minutes

Cinnamon rolls are a special treat at our house. One day, with leftover toasted pecans, we decided to experiment—and this version was born.

2 cups all-purpose flour, plus more
    for dusting

2 tablespoons granulated sugar, plus
    ¼ cup, divided

1 teaspoon salt

3 tablespoons butter, at room temperature

¾ cup milk, whole or 2%

¼ cup packed light brown sugar

½ cup chopped pecans, toasted

1 to 2 tablespoons oil

¼ cup confectioners' sugar (optional)

1. In a large bowl, whisk the flour, 2 tablespoons granulated sugar, and salt until blended. Stir in the butter and milk briefly until a sticky dough forms.
2. In a small bowl, stir together the brown sugar and remaining ¼ cup of granulated sugar.
3. Place a piece of parchment paper on a work surface and dust it with flour. Roll the dough on the prepared surface to ¼ inch thickness.
4. Spread the sugar mixture over the dough. Sprinkle the pecans on top. Roll up the dough jelly roll–style, pinching the ends to seal. Cut the dough into 12 rolls.
5. Preheat the air fryer to 320°F.
6. Line the air fryer tray with parchment paper and spritz the parchment with oil. Place 6 rolls on the prepared parchment.
7. Bake for 5 minutes. Flip the rolls and bake for 5 to 7 minutes more until lightly browned. Repeat with the remaining rolls.
8. Sprinkle with confectioners' sugar (if using).

◆ **Glazed Pecan Rolls:** In a medium bowl and using a handheld electric mixer, beat 3 ounces cream cheese (at room temperature) 1 cup confectioners' sugar, and 2 tablespoons bourbon until blended. Spread 1 teaspoon of glaze over each roll.

Per Serving (1 roll): Calories: 194; Total fat: 8g; Saturated fat: 2.5g; Cholesterol: 9mg; Sodium: 203mg; Carbohydrates: 28g; Fiber: 1g; Protein: 3g

APPLE ROLLS

FAMILY FAVORITE

Makes: 12 rolls · **Prep:** 20 minutes · **Fry time:** 20 to 24 minutes

Ellijay, a small town nestled in the mountains, is Georgia's apple capital. From August to December, tourists flock to u-pick farms for the bounty. This recipe lets you celebrate apples year-round.

FOR THE APPLE ROLLS

2 cups all-purpose flour, plus more
    for dusting

2 tablespoons granulated sugar

1 teaspoon salt

3 tablespoons butter, at room temperature

¾ cup milk, whole or 2%

½ cup packed light brown sugar

1 teaspoon ground cinnamon

1 large Granny Smith apple, peeled
    and diced

1 to 2 tablespoons oil

FOR THE ICING

½ cup confectioners' sugar

½ teaspoon vanilla extract

2 to 3 tablespoons milk, whole or 2%

TO MAKE THE APPLE ROLLS

1. In a large bowl, whisk the flour, granulated sugar, and salt until blended. Stir in the butter and milk briefly until a sticky dough forms.
2. In a small bowl, stir together the brown sugar, cinnamon, and apple.
3. Place a piece of parchment paper on a work surface and dust it with flour. Roll the dough on the prepared surface to ¼ inch thickness.
4. Spread the apple mixture over the dough. Roll up the dough jelly roll–style, pinching the ends to seal. Cut the dough into 12 rolls.
5. Preheat the air fryer to 320°F.
6. Line the air fryer tray with parchment paper and spritz it with oil. Place 6 rolls on the prepared parchment.
7. Bake for 5 minutes. Flip the rolls and bake for 5 to 7 minutes more until lightly browned. Repeat with the remaining rolls.

TO MAKE THE ICING

8. In a medium bowl, whisk the confectioners' sugar, vanilla, and milk until blended.

9. Drizzle over the warm rolls.

◆ **Caramel-Apple Rolls:** Stir 1 tablespoon caramel sauce into the apple mixture in step 2.

Per Serving (1 roll): Calories: 195; Total fat: 5g; Saturated fat: 2.5g; Cholesterol: 9mg; Sodium: 205mg; Carbohydrates: 35g; Fiber: 1g; Protein: 3g

HASH BROWN CASSEROLE

FAMILY FAVORITE

Serves: 4 · **Prep:** 15 minutes · **Fry time:** 30 minutes

The first recipe for "hashed and browned potatoes" was written by Maria Parloa and appeared in her 1887 Kitchen Companion. *Our recipe adds a Southern touch, turning hash browns into a casserole—something you're always sure to find on the table in this part of the country.*

3½ cups frozen hash browns

1 teaspoon salt

1 teaspoon freshly ground black pepper

3 tablespoons butter, melted

1 (10.5-ounce) can cream of chicken soup

½ cup sour cream

1 cup minced onion

½ cup shredded sharp Cheddar cheese

1 to 2 tablespoons oil

1. Place the frozen hash browns in a large bowl and sprinkle with the salt and pepper. Stir in the melted butter, cream of chicken soup, and sour cream until blended. Stir in the onion and Cheddar cheese.
2. Preheat the air fryer to 325°F. Spritz a 6-inch air fryer–safe pan with oil.
3. Add the hash brown mixture to the prepared pan and place it on the air fryer tray.
4. Cook for 30 minutes, stirring every 10 minutes. The mixture will be slightly soupy when it is finished cooking. Let sit for 5 minutes before eating.

♦ **Bacon-Chive Hash Brown Casserole:** Add 3 chopped cooked bacon slices and 1 tablespoon finely chopped fresh chives to the mixture in step 1.

Per Serving: Calories: 664; Total fat: 49g; Saturated fat: 16g; Cholesterol: 63mg; Sodium: 1,944mg; Carbohydrates: 48g; Fiber: 4g; Protein: 9g

CHAPTER FOUR

~

SIZZLING SNACKS AND APPETIZERS

STUFFED FRIED MUSHROOMS

NEW TRADITION

Serves: 10 · **Prep:** 20 minutes · **Fry time:** 10 to 11 minutes

Panko bread crumbs are the preferred choice for the air fryer. They come in two varieties (white and tan) and are larger and flakier than traditional bread crumbs. They also absorb less oil and stay crisper in the fryer for a longer period of time.

½ cup panko bread crumbs
½ teaspoon freshly ground black pepper
½ teaspoon onion powder
½ teaspoon cayenne pepper

1 (8-ounce) package cream cheese, at room temperature
20 cremini or button mushrooms, stemmed
1 to 2 tablespoons oil

1. In a medium bowl, whisk the bread crumbs, black pepper, onion powder, and cayenne until blended.
2. Add the cream cheese and mix until well blended. Fill each mushroom top with 1 teaspoon of the cream cheese mixture
3. Preheat the air fryer to 360°F. Line the air fryer tray with a piece of parchment paper.
4. Place the mushrooms on the parchment and spritz with oil.
5. Cook for 5 minutes. Shake the basket and cook for 5 to 6 minutes more until the filling is firm and the mushrooms are soft.

◆ **Southern Know-How:** For an easy, flavorful stuffing for chicken breasts, finely chop the leftover mushroom stems. In a small skillet over medium-high heat, sauté the stems in 1 tablespoon butter with 2 teaspoons minced garlic for 2 minutes. Stir the sautéed mixture into 1 cup panko bread crumbs.

Per Serving (2 mushrooms): Calories: 120; Total fat: 9.5g; Saturated fat: 5g; Cholesterol: 23mg; Sodium: 162mg; Carbohydrates: 7g; Fiber: 0g; Protein: 3g

SAUSAGE BALLS

FAMILY FAVORITE

Serves: 8 · **Prep:** 10 minutes · **Fry time:** 10 to 11 minutes

Brittany is a huge fan of sausage balls. At the annual church Christmas party, our friend Cheryl would always bring an extra dish of sausage balls just for her. Our version has cream cheese for added flavor.

1½ cups baking mix, such as Bisquick

12 ounces mild ground sausage

1 cup shredded mild Cheddar cheese

3 ounces cream cheese, at room temperature

1 to 2 tablespoons oil

1. In a large bowl, combine the baking mix, ground sausage, Cheddar cheese, and cream cheese. Using clean hands, mix until the dough is combined. Roll the dough into about 16 (1-inch) balls.
2. Preheat the air fryer to 325°F. Line the air fryer tray with parchment paper.
3. Place the sausage balls on the parchment and spritz with oil.
4. Cook for 5 minutes. Shake the basket and cook for 5 to 6 minutes more until lightly brown, firm, and crisp.

♦ **Spice It Up:** Omit the Cheddar cheese. Substitute hot sausage for the mild sausage and stir in 1 teaspoon red pepper flakes and 1 cup shredded pepper Jack cheese.

Per Serving (2 sausage balls): Calories: 333; Total fat: 24g; Saturated fat: 9.5g; Cholesterol: 61mg; Sodium: 705mg; Carbohydrates: 17g; Fiber: 0.5g; Protein: 13g

FRIED GREEN TOMATOES AND DIPPING SAUCE

NEW TRADITION

Serves: 4 • **Prep:** 1 hour 20 minutes • **Fry time:** 10 to 12 minutes

Fried green tomatoes (as seen on the cover of this book) are considered a Southern delicacy. According to food historian Robert F. Moss, the dish originated from the Northeast and Midwest. Home economics teachers are credited with spreading it to the South.

FOR THE DIPPING SAUCE
¾ cup mayonnaise
1 tablespoon minced garlic
1 tablespoon freshly squeezed lemon juice
½ teaspoon salt
½ teaspoon freshly ground black pepper

FOR THE FRIED GREEN TOMATOES
1½ cups All-Purpose Breading (page 18)
1 teaspoon Creole Seasoning (page 16)
2 large eggs, beaten
1½ cups yellow cornmeal
3 green tomatoes, thinly sliced
1 to 2 tablespoons oil

TO MAKE THE DIPPING SAUCE
1. In a small bowl, whisk the mayonnaise, garlic, lemon juice, salt, and pepper until blended.
2. Cover and refrigerate for 1 hour.

TO MAKE THE FRIED GREEN TOMATOES
3. In a shallow bowl, stir together the All-Purpose Breading and Creole Seasoning. Place the beaten eggs in a second shallow bowl and the cornmeal in a third.
4. Pat the tomatoes dry. One at a time, dip the tomatoes in the breading, the eggs, and the cornmeal, coating thoroughly.
5. Preheat the air fryer to 400°F. Line the air fryer with parchment paper.

6. Place the coated tomatoes on the parchment and lightly spritz them with oil.
7. Cook for 5 minutes. Flip the tomatoes, spritz with oil, and cook for 5 to 7 minutes more until lightly browned and crispy, depending on the thickness of the slices. Serve with the dipping sauce.

♦ **Southern Know-How:** Green tomatoes are tomatoes that have not fully ripened. Choose those that are firm, not hard, and 1 to 2 inches wide.

Per Serving: Calories: 614; Total fat: 37g; Saturated fat: 6g; Cholesterol: 79mg; Sodium: 916mg; Carbohydrates: 58g; Fiber: 3.5g; Protein: 9g

FRIED PICKLES

NEW TRADITION

Serves: 5 • **Prep:** 20 minutes • **Fry time:** 7 minutes

First served in Atkins, Arkansas, at the Duchess Drive-In in 1963, fried pickles were the brainchild of Bernell "Fatman" Austin. His recipe is a closely guarded family secret, but you can still try it at the Atkins Pickle Festival each May. Look for hamburger dill pickle chips in the pickle section of the grocery store. We like Vlasic or Heinz.

¼ cup mayonnaise

2 tablespoons ketchup

1 teaspoon prepared horseradish

¼ teaspoon Creole Seasoning (page 16)

1¼ cups All-Purpose Breading (page 18)

2 large eggs, beaten

¼ cup beer

1½ cups panko bread crumbs

20 hamburger dill pickle chips

1 to 2 tablespoons oil

1. In a small bowl, whisk the mayonnaise, ketchup, horseradish, and Creole Seasoning until blended. This sauce can be made ahead and refrigerated for the flavors to blend.
2. Place the All-Purpose Breading in a shallow bowl, whisk together the eggs and beer in a second shallow bowl, and place the bread crumbs in a third shallow bowl.
3. One at a time, dip each pickle in the breading, the eggs, and the bread crumbs, coating thoroughly.
4. Preheat the air fryer to 375°F. Place a piece of parchment paper on the air fryer tray.
5. Place the pickles on the parchment and spritz with oil.
6. Cook for 3 minutes. Shake the basket and spritz the pickles with oil. Cook for 4 minutes more until lightly browned and crispy. Serve with the sauce.

♦ **Spice It Up:** Add an extra 1 teaspoon Creole Seasoning (page 16) to the breading.

Per Serving (4 pickles): Calories: 278; Total fat: 13g; Saturated fat: 2g; Cholesterol: 54mg; Sodium: 1,316mg; Carbohydrates: 33g; Fiber: 0.5g; Protein: 5g

BUTTERMILK ONION RINGS

TRUE CLASSIC

Serves: 4 • **Prep:** 1 hour • **Fry time:** 8 minutes

Air-fried onion rings paired with bold sauces produce mouthwatering flavors without the grease. Try these with the Hot Honey Mustard Dip (page 19) or Spicy Garlic Honey Mustard Dip (page 19).

2 yellow onions, cut into ¼-inch-thick slices
1½ cups buttermilk
2 cups All-Purpose Breading (page 18)

2 large eggs, beaten
2 cups panko bread crumbs
1 to 2 tablespoons oil

1. In a large bowl, combine the onion rings and buttermilk, making sure the onions are completely covered. Let soak for at least 1 hour, or overnight.
2. Place the All-Purpose Breading in a shallow bowl, the beaten eggs in a second shallow bowl, and the bread crumbs in a third shallow bowl.
3. One at a time, dip the onion rings in the breading, the eggs, and the bread crumbs, coating thoroughly.
4. Preheat the air fryer to 375°F. Line the air fryer tray with parchment paper.
5. Place the onions on the parchment and spritz with oil.
6. Cook for 4 minutes. Shake the basket, spritz the onions with oil again, and cook for 4 minutes more until lightly browned and crispy.

◆ **Southern Know-How:** Yellow onions are sweeter than other varieties. If you'd like a true Southern onion, consider the Vidalia. They are only grown in a few counties in Southern Georgia and are trademarked by the Vidalia Onion Act of 1986.

Per Serving: Calories: 318; Total fat: 7g; Saturated fat: 1g; Cholesterol: 63mg; Sodium: 880mg; Carbohydrates: 54g; Fiber: 2g; Protein: 9g

CHEESY CORN BREAD

NEW TRADITION

Serves: 6 • **Prep:** 20 minutes • **Fry time:** 15 to 20 minutes

Everyone in the South has a "secret" family recipe for corn bread. Some people swear by shortening, whereas others prefer butter. Some change the flour and cornmeal ratios. We took our classic family recipe and added two of our favorite ingredients: bacon and cheese.

---

1 cup self-rising yellow cornmeal

½ cup self-rising flour

8 tablespoons (1 stick) butter, melted

1 large egg, beaten

1 cup buttermilk

3 bacon slices, air-fried (page 3) and crumbled

½ cup shredded mild Cheddar cheese

1 to 2 tablespoons oil

1. In a medium bowl, whisk the cornmeal and flour until blended.
2. Add the melted butter and egg and stir until moistened.
3. Add the buttermilk and stir until blended.
4. Stir in the cooked bacon and Cheddar cheese.
5. Preheat the air fryer to 360°F. Spritz a 6-inch air fryer–safe pan with oil.
6. Pour the corn bread batter into the prepared pan.
7. Cook for 8 minutes. Stir the batter and cook for 7 to 12 minutes more, or until a toothpick inserted into the center comes out clean.

♦ **Spice It Up:** Replace the Cheddar cheese with shredded pepper Jack cheese and add 2 tablespoons chopped jalapeño pepper and ½ cup corn kernels to the batter in step 4.

Per Serving: Calories: 362; Total fat: 22g; Saturated fat: 13g; Cholesterol: 88mg; Sodium: 733mg; Carbohydrates: 31g; Fiber: 2g; Protein: 10g

DEVILED EGGS

TRUE CLASSIC

Serves: 12 · **Prep:** 20 minutes · **Fry time:** 16 minutes

You'll find a plate of deviled eggs (pictured on page 34) in attendance at any church dinner, potluck, or family reunion in the South. Famed North Carolina chef Aaron Deal says, "A real Southern girl should own an iced-tea pitcher and a deviled-egg plate." Pam owns four.

3 cups ice

12 large eggs

½ cup mayonnaise

10 hamburger dill pickle chips, diced

¼ cup diced onion

2 teaspoons yellow mustard

2 teaspoons salt

1 teaspoon freshly ground black pepper

½ teaspoon paprika

1. Preheat the air fryer to 250°F. Place the ice in a large bowl.
2. Place the eggs on the air fryer tray.
3. Cook for 16 minutes. Remove the eggs and immediately submerge them in the ice. Let cool.
4. Peel the eggs. Halve them lengthwise and scoop the egg yolks into a small bowl. Add the mayonnaise, pickles, onion, mustard, salt, and pepper. Using a fork, mash until blended.
5. Spoon 1 to 2 teaspoons of the egg yolk mixture into each egg white half.
6. Sprinkle each filled egg with a dash of paprika.

◆ **Southern Know-How:** You can make hard-boiled eggs in advance and keep them refrigerated for up to 7 days. To make a perfect egg half, use unwaxed dental floss to halve the eggs.

Per Serving (2 egg halves): Calories: 136; Total fat: 12g; Saturated fat: 2.5g; Cholesterol: 190mg; Sodium: 656mg; Carbohydrates: 1g; Fiber: 0g; Protein: 6g

HUSHPUPPIES

TRUE CLASSIC

Serves: 12 · **Prep:** 45 minutes · **Fry time:** 10 minutes

Pam first tried these hushpuppies at Catfish Cabin in Albertville, Alabama, when she was a child. They're billed as "to die for," and Pam couldn't wait to attempt her own version. For added spice, increase the jalapeños to 4 teaspoons.

1 cup self-rising yellow cornmeal

½ cup all-purpose flour

1 teaspoon sugar

1 teaspoon salt

1 teaspoon freshly ground black pepper

1 large egg

⅓ cup canned creamed corn

1 cup minced onion

2 teaspoons minced jalapeño pepper

1 to 2 tablespoons oil

1. In a large bowl, whisk the cornmeal, flour, sugar, salt, and pepper until blended.
2. In a small bowl, stir together the egg and creamed corn. Add the egg mixture to the cornmeal mixture and stir until blended. Stir in the onion and jalapeño. Cover and refrigerate for 30 minutes before frying.
3. Preheat the air fryer to 375°F. Line the air fryer tray with parchment paper and brush it lightly with oil.
4. Shape the batter into about 24 (1-inch) balls. Working in batches, place them on the prepared parchment, leaving space between the hushpuppies.
5. Cook for 5 minutes. Shake the basket and brush the hushpuppies with oil again, if desired. Cook for 5 minutes more until lightly browned.

◆ **Squash Puppies:** Omit the jalapeño and creamed corn. Stir in ½ cup finely diced squash. Let the batter rest for 1 hour in the refrigerator before frying.

Per Serving (2 hushpuppies): Calories: 81; Total fat: 2g; Saturated fat: 0.5g; Cholesterol: 15mg; Sodium: 363mg; Carbohydrates: 15g; Fiber: 1g; Protein: 2g

CHAPTER FIVE

~

GREENS 'N' BEANS

COLLARD GREENS AND BEAN SOUP

NEW TRADITION

Serves: 4 • **Prep:** 10 minutes • **Fry time:** 30 minutes

In the South, eating "a mess of" collard greens on New Year's Day is said to bring good luck. Pam prefers hers in soup (pictured on page 46).

1 (14.5-ounce) can diced tomatoes

1 teaspoon Italian-Style Seasoning (page 17)

1 teaspoon salt

1 teaspoon freshly ground black pepper

¼ teaspoon red pepper flakes

¼ cup diced mild sweet onion

½ (15-ounce) can chickpeas, drained and rinsed

1 teaspoon minced garlic

1 cup packed finely chopped collard greens

2 tablespoons sugar

5 cups chicken broth, divided

1 tablespoon cornstarch

3 bacon slices, air-fried (page 3) and chopped

¼ cup grated Parmesan cheese (optional)

1. In a large bowl, stir together the tomatoes with their juices, Italian-Style Seasoning, salt, pepper, and red pepper flakes until blended. Stir in the onion, chickpeas, garlic, collards, sugar, and 2 cups of chicken broth.
2. Preheat the air fryer to 400°F.
3. Pour the collard mixture into a 9-inch square air fryer–safe pan and place it on the air fryer tray.
4. Cook for 10 minutes. Stir. Add 1 cup of chicken broth. Cook for 10 minutes more, stir, and add 1 cup of chicken broth.

5. In a small bowl, whisk the cornstarch and remaining 1 cup of chicken broth until dissolved. Add this slurry to the soup and stir to combine. Cook for 10 minutes more.
6. Serve topped with bacon crumbles and Parmesan cheese (if using).

♦ **Southern Know-How:** Quick reminder: To cook bacon in an air fryer, preheat the air fryer to 375°F. Place 8 bacon slices on the air fryer tray. Cook for 5 to 6 minutes. Flip and cook for 5 to 6 minutes more, depending on the degree of crispness desired.

Per Serving: *Calories: 157; Total fat: 3.5g; Saturated fat: 1g; Cholesterol: 12mg; Sodium: 2,074mg; Carbohydrates: 23g; Fiber: 3.5g; Protein: 7g*

FRIED OKRA

TRUE CLASSIC

Serves: 4 · **Prep:** 15 minutes · **Fry time:** 8 to 10 minutes

Okra, a popular dish in Africa, is thought to have been brought to the South in the 1700s by enslaved persons. Used as a thickening agent in cooking by the Creoles and Cajuns, its popularity soon spread. This versatile vegetable can be sautéed, stewed, pickled, boiled, or fried.

---

1 cup self-rising yellow cornmeal

1 teaspoon Italian-Style Seasoning (page 17)

1 teaspoon paprika

1 teaspoon salt

½ teaspoon freshly ground black pepper

2 large eggs, beaten

2 cups okra slices (¼ inch thick)

1 to 2 tablespoons oil

1. In a shallow bowl, whisk the cornmeal, Italian-Style Seasoning, paprika, salt, and pepper until blended. Place the beaten eggs in a second shallow bowl.
2. Add the okra to the beaten egg and stir to coat. Add the egg and okra mixture to the cornmeal mixture and stir until coated.
3. Preheat the air fryer to 400°F. Line the air fryer tray with parchment paper.
4. Place the okra on the parchment and spritz it with oil.
5. Cook for 4 minutes. Shake the basket, spritz the okra with oil, and cook for 4 to 6 minutes more until lightly browned and crispy.

♦ **Southern Know-How:** When choosing okra, look for bright green pods that feel firm. Avoid okra more than 4 inches in length, as it tends to be tough.

Per Serving: Calories: 137; Total fat: 5.5g; Saturated fat: 1g; Cholesterol: 61mg; Sodium: 698mg; Carbohydrates: 19g; Fiber: 2g; Protein: 5g

CANDIED SWEET POTATOES

FAMILY FAVORITE

Serves: 4 · **Prep:** 15 minutes · **Fry time:** 10 minutes

Are sweet potatoes and yams the same? According to the USDA, they are in the United States. Any product marketed as a "yam" must include "sweet potato" on the packaging. However, yams are a different species, related to the lily family, that is native to Asia and Africa.

2 tablespoons butter, melted

1 tablespoon light brown sugar

2 sweet potatoes, peeled and cut into ½-inch cubes

1 to 2 tablespoons oil

1. In a medium bowl, stir together the melted butter and brown sugar until blended. Toss the sweet potatoes in the butter mixture until coated.
2. Preheat the air fryer to 400°F. Line the air fryer tray with parchment paper.
3. Place the sweet potatoes on the parchment and spritz with oil.
4. Cook for 5 minutes. Shake the basket, spritz the sweet potatoes with oil, and cook for 5 minutes more until they're soft enough to cut with a fork.

♦ **Spice It Up:** Omit the brown sugar. Add ½ teaspoon onion powder, ½ teaspoon chili powder, and ⅛ teaspoon cayenne to the melted butter. Proceed with the recipe as directed.

Per Serving: Calories: 150; Total fat: 9g; Saturated fat: 4g; Cholesterol: 15mg; Sodium: 38mg; Carbohydrates: 16g; Fiber: 2g; Protein: 1g

CORN FRITTERS

TRUE CLASSIC

Serves: 6 · **Prep:** 15 minutes · **Fry time:** 8 minutes

This classic corn fritter allows the flavor of the corn to shine through. It's good served with a meal or brushed with butter, lightly sprinkled with powdered sugar, and served as dessert.

1 cup self-rising flour
1 tablespoon sugar
1 teaspoon salt
1 large egg, lightly beaten

¼ cup buttermilk
¾ cup corn kernels (fresh or canned)
¼ cup minced onion
1 to 2 tablespoons oil

1. In a medium bowl, whisk the flour, sugar, and salt until blended. Stir in the egg and buttermilk. Add the corn and minced onion. Mix well. Shape the corn fritter batter into 12 balls.
2. Preheat the air fryer to 350°F. Line the air fryer tray with parchment paper.
3. Place the fritters on the parchment and spritz with oil.
4. Cook for 4 minutes.
5. Flip the fritters, spritz them with oil, and cook for 4 minutes more until firm and lightly browned.

♦ **Spice It Up:** Add 1 teaspoon chili powder to the flour mixture and 1 cup pepper Jack cheese and 1 jalapeño pepper, diced, with the corn and onion.

Per Serving (2 fritters): Calories: 136; Total fat: 3.5g; Saturated fat: 0.5g; Cholesterol: 32mg; Sodium: 671mg; Carbohydrates: 22g; Fiber: 1g; Protein: 4g

SOUTHERN POTATO CAKES

FAMILY FAVORITE

Serves: 6 · **Prep:** 45 to 55 minutes · **Fry time:** 10 minutes

When Pam was a child, she looked forward to mashed potatoes for dinner. In her family of three, leftover potatoes were the norm, and she knew they'd appear the next day as potato cakes. She adapted this family recipe, adding bacon for extra flavor and bread crumbs for thickening.

4 medium russet potatoes

1 large egg

½ cup shredded Cheddar cheese

½ cup minced onion

4 bacon slices, air-fried (page 3) and diced

¾ cup panko bread crumbs

1 to 2 tablespoons oil

1. Preheat the air fryer to 390°F. Cut several thin slits in each potato. Brush with oil, and place them in the air fryer basket to cook for 30 to 40 minutes, until soft.
2. Move the potatoes to a large bowl, and mash. Stir in the egg, cheese, onion, and bacon until blended. Stir in the bread crumbs. Shape the mixture into 12 balls.
3. Adjust the air fryer temperature to 350°F. Line the air fryer tray with parchment paper.
4. Place the potato balls on the parchment and gently press them with a fork to flatten slightly. Spritz the potato cakes with oil.
5. Cook for 5 minutes. Flip the cakes, spritz them with oil, and cook for 5 more minutes until lightly browned and crispy.

◆ **Make It Vegetarian:** Simply omit the bacon. To make up for the flavor boost, try swapping in sweet potatoes for the russets.

Per Serving (2 potato cakes): Calories: 223; Total fat: 8.5g; Saturated fat: 3g; Cholesterol: 45mg; Sodium: 383mg; Carbohydrates: 29g; Fiber: 1.5g; Protein: 8g

CORN CUSTARD

FAMILY FAVORITE

Serves: 4 • **Prep:** 10 minutes • **Fry time:** 20 minutes

This creamy corn custard is down-home comfort food. Sometimes called corn pudding or corn casserole, in our version the custard is not fully firm. It's a wonderful accompaniment to any type of meat dish and can be adapted for any taste.

1 (14.5-ounce) can creamed corn
½ cup sour cream
1 tablespoon butter, melted
1 teaspoon onion powder
1 teaspoon salt

½ teaspoon freshly ground black pepper
1 large egg
2 tablespoons cornstarch
1 to 2 tablespoons oil

1. In a medium bowl, stir together the creamed corn, sour cream, melted butter, onion powder, salt, and pepper.
2. In a small bowl, whisk together the egg and cornstarch. Add the egg mixture to the corn mixture and stir to combine.
3. Preheat the air fryer to 320°F. Spritz a 6-inch air fryer–safe pan with oil.
4. Pour the corn mixture into the prepared pan and place it on the air fryer tray.
5. Cook for 20 minutes, stirring the mixture every 5 minutes, until firm on top but with a creamy center.

♦ **Ham and Cheese Custard:** Add ¼ to ½ cup finely diced cooked ham and 1 cup shredded Cheddar cheese in step 2.

Per Serving: Calories: 198; Total fat: 17g; Saturated fat: 5.5g; Cholesterol: 74mg; Sodium: 911mg; Carbohydrates: 17g; Fiber: 1.5g; Protein: 3g

ZUCCHINI-PARMESAN FRIES

NEW TRADITION

Serves: 4 • **Prep:** 20 minutes • **Fry time:** 16 to 20 minutes

The largest zucchini ever grown, as recorded by the Guinness Book of World Records, *was more than 8 feet long, whereas the heaviest weighed 64 pounds, 8 ounces. Unless you're going for a record, zucchini is best picked and used at 6 to 8 inches long.*

---

1 cup yellow cornmeal

1 teaspoon Creole Seasoning (page 16)

1 teaspoon salt

½ teaspoon freshly ground black pepper

2 large eggs, beaten

¼ cup grated Parmesan cheese

1½ cups panko bread crumbs

2 zucchini, peeled and cut into 1-inch-thick strips

1 to 2 tablespoons oil

1. In a shallow dish, whisk the cornmeal, Creole Seasoning, salt, and pepper until blended. Place the beaten eggs in a second shallow bowl, and stir together the Parmesan cheese and bread crumbs in a third bowl.
2. One at a time, dip the zucchini into the cornmeal, the beaten eggs, and the bread crumbs, coating thoroughly.
3. Preheat the air fryer to 350°F. Line the air fryer tray with parchment paper.
4. Place half the zucchini fries on the parchment and spritz with oil.
5. Cook for 4 minutes. Shake the basket, spritz the fries with oil, and cook for 4 to 6 minutes more until lightly browned and crispy. Repeat with the remaining fries.

♦ **Southern Know-How:** Keep zucchini fresh by refrigerating it, unwashed, in a plastic bag, where it will keep for up to 5 days. Discard any mushy, discolored zucchini.

Per Serving: Calories: 281; Total fat: 7.5g; Saturated fat: 1.5g; Cholesterol: 65mg; Sodium: 920mg; Carbohydrates: 44g; Fiber: 2g; Protein: 8g

GREEN BEANS WITH BACON

NEW TRADITION

Serves: 4 · **Prep:** 15 minutes · **Fry time:** 8 to 10 minutes

Pam grew up spending summers on her grandparents' farm. On Sunday afternoons, while the family visited, grocery sacks full of freshly picked green beans were dragged to the porch. Everyone would talk while stringing and snapping beans. Pam tried to escape these chores, usually without success, and still prefers snapping smaller amounts of beans.

1 to 2 tablespoons oil

2 (14.5-ounce) cans cut green beans, drained

4 bacon slices, air-fried (page 3) and diced

¼ cup minced onion

1 tablespoon distilled white vinegar

1 teaspoon freshly squeezed lemon juice

½ teaspoon salt

½ teaspoon freshly ground black pepper

1. Spritz a 6-inch air fryer–safe pan with oil. In the prepared pan, stir together the green beans, bacon, onion, vinegar, lemon juice, salt, and pepper until blended.
2. Preheat the air fryer to 370°F.
3. Place the pan on the air fryer tray.
4. Cook for 4 minutes. Stir the green beans and cook for 4 to 6 minutes more until soft.

◆ **Make It Vegetarian:** Omit the salt and bacon. Stir in 1 teaspoon red pepper flakes, 1 teaspoon garlic powder, ½ teaspoon seasoning salt, and ¼ cup finely chopped veggie bacon.

Per Serving: Calories: 84; Total fat: 6.5g; Saturated fat: 1.5g; Cholesterol: 8mg; Sodium: 584mg; Carbohydrates: 3g; Fiber: 1.5g; Protein: 3g

CHAPTER SIX

∼

CRISPY FISH AND SEAFOOD

SALMON PATTIES

TRUE CLASSIC

Serves: 4 · **Prep:** 10 minutes · **Fry time:** 8 to 12 minutes

Croquettes, as they are known in other parts of the world, were once frequently served on Southern dinner tables. Even famed author William Faulkner was a fan, although his cook's recipe supposedly called for the addition of pickle relish and saltine crackers.

2 (5-ounce) cans salmon, flaked
2 large eggs, beaten
⅓ cup minced onion
⅔ cup panko bread crumbs
1½ teaspoons Italian-Style Seasoning
   (page 17)

1 teaspoon garlic powder
1 to 2 tablespoons oil
Pecan Tartar Sauce (page 21)

1. In a medium bowl, stir together the salmon, eggs, and onion.
2. In a small bowl, whisk the bread crumbs, Italian-Style Seasoning, and garlic powder until blended. Add the bread crumb mixture to the salmon mixture and stir until blended. Shape the mixture into 8 patties.
3. Preheat the air fryer to 350°F. Line the air fryer tray with parchment paper.
4. Working in batches as needed, place the patties on the parchment and spritz with oil.
5. Cook for 4 minutes. Flip, spritz the patties with oil, and cook for 4 to 8 minutes more, until browned and firm.
6. Serve with Pecan Tartar Sauce.

◆ **Tuna Patties:** Omit the salmon and substitute 2 (5-ounce) cans of tuna and add 2 tablespoons of pickle relish.

Per Serving (2 salmon patties): Calories: 514; Total fat: 39g; Saturated fat: 8.5g; Cholesterol: 163mg; Sodium: 785mg; Carbohydrates: 19g; Fiber: 1.5g; Protein: 22g

FRIED SHRIMP

TRUE CLASSIC

Serves: 4 · **Prep:** 15 minutes · **Fry time:** 5 minutes

If you're landlocked, like we are, purchase frozen shrimp instead of fresh shrimp at your local supermarket seafood counter. Most fresh shrimp you find at grocery stores were shipped frozen, then thawed at the store. Keep the shrimp frozen until ready to use.

½ cup self-rising flour

1 teaspoon paprika

1 teaspoon salt

½ teaspoon freshly ground black pepper

1 large egg, beaten

1 cup finely crushed panko bread crumbs

20 frozen large shrimp (about 1 pound), peeled and deveined

1 to 2 tablespoons oil

Pecan Tartar Sauce (page 21)

1. In a shallow bowl, whisk the flour, paprika, salt, and pepper until blended. Add the beaten egg to a second shallow bowl and the bread crumbs to a third.
2. One at a time, dip the shrimp into the flour, the egg, and the bread crumbs, coating thoroughly.
3. Preheat the air fryer to 400°F. Line the air fryer tray with parchment paper.
4. Place the shrimp on the parchment and spritz with oil.
5. Cook for 2 minutes. Shake the basket, spritz the shrimp with oil, and cook for 3 minutes more until lightly browned and crispy.
6. Serve with Pecan Tartar Sauce.

♦ **Southern Know-How:** Make an easy cocktail sauce: Mix 1¼ cups chili sauce, 1 tablespoon creamed horseradish, 1 tablespoon Worcestershire sauce, 1 teaspoon freshly squeezed lemon juice, and ½ teaspoon freshly ground black pepper. Chill before serving.

Per Serving (5 shrimp): Calories: 524; Total fat: 37g; Saturated fat: 7.5g; Cholesterol: 205mg; Sodium: 1,685mg; Carbohydrates: 26g; Fiber: 1.5g; Protein: 21g

BLACKENED FISH

NEW TRADITION

Serves: 4 · **Prep:** 15 minutes · **Fry time:** 8 to 10 minutes

Want your batter or coating to stick? Make sure the food item being coated is dry before dipping it in the egg mixture. Ingredients can be gently patted with a paper towel to ensure dryness.

---

1 large egg, beaten
Blackened Seasoning (page 17)
2 tablespoons light brown sugar

4 (4-ounce) tilapia fillets
1 to 2 tablespoons oil

1. In a shallow bowl, place the beaten egg. In a second shallow bowl, stir together the Blackened Seasoning and the brown sugar.
2. One at a time, dip the fish fillets in the egg, then the brown sugar mixture, coating thoroughly.
3. Preheat the air fryer to 300°F. Line the air fryer tray with parchment paper.
4. Place the coated fish on the parchment and spritz with oil.
5. Cook for 4 minutes. Flip the fish, spritz it with oil, and cook for 4 to 6 minutes more until the fish is white inside and flakes easily with a fork.

♦ **Variation:** Catfish and even salmon are excellent and tasty swaps if tilapia isn't available at the fish counter.

Per Serving: Calories: 193; Total fat: 7g; Saturated fat: 1.5g; Cholesterol: 79mg; Sodium: 1,227mg; Carbohydrates: 9g; Fiber: 1g; Protein: 24g

NASHVILLE HOT FISH

NEW TRADITION

Serves: 4 · **Prep:** 20 minutes · **Fry time:** 8 to 10 minutes

This is the fish version of the popular Nashville hot chicken, originally created by Thornton Prince. The story goes that Prince, who was quite the ladies' man, had one lady not happy with the arrangement. Intent on revenge, she served him this dish. Instead of suffering, he enjoyed it so much that he recreated the recipe and opened the BBQ Chicken Shack restaurant.

1 cup Nashville Hot Breading (page 18)

1 teaspoon chili powder

2 large eggs, beaten

2 tablespoons hot sauce, plus more for serving (optional)

1 cup panko bread crumbs

4 (4-ounce) tilapia fillets

1 to 2 tablespoons oil

1. In a shallow bowl, stir together the Nashville Hot Breading and chili powder. In a second shallow bowl, whisk the eggs and hot sauce until combined, and place the bread crumbs in a third bowl.
2. One at a time, dip the fillets in the breading, the eggs, and in the bread crumbs, coating thoroughly.
3. Preheat the air fryer to 300°F. Line the air fryer tray with parchment paper.
4. Place the coated fish on the parchment and spritz with oil.
5. Cook for 4 minutes. Flip the fish, spritz it with oil, and cook for 4 to 6 minutes more until the fish is white inside and flakes easily with a fork.

♦ **Nashville Hot Chicken:** Substitute 1 pound boneless, skinless chicken breasts for the tilapia. Increase the cooking temperature to 360°F. Bake for 8 minutes. Turn the chicken, spritz with oil, and bake for 7 to 12 minutes more, or until the internal temperature is 165°F and the juices run clear.

Per Serving: Calories: 303; Total fat: 8g; Saturated fat: 2g; Cholesterol: 110mg; Sodium: 533mg; Carbohydrates: 29g; Fiber: 0.5g; Protein: 28g

OYSTER PO'BOY

TRUE CLASSIC

Serves: 4 · **Prep:** 20 minutes · **Fry time:** 5 minutes

In the sleepy fishing village of Yscloskey, Louisiana, oyster producers have found a use for the leftover concrete rubble from Hurricane Katrina. The rubble is crushed and used to seed oyster beds. The spat (baby oysters) stick more readily to these beds. This way, growers can produce oysters in just two years instead of the normal five.

¾ cup All-Purpose Breading (page 18)

¼ cup yellow cornmeal

1 tablespoon Cajun Seasoning (page 16)

1 teaspoon salt

2 large eggs, beaten

1 teaspoon hot sauce

1 pound (about 12 large) pre-shucked oysters

1 to 2 tablespoons oil

1 (12-inch) French baguette, quartered and sliced horizontally

Pecan Tartar Sauce (page 21)

2 cups shredded lettuce, divided

2 tomatoes, cut into slices

1. In a shallow bowl, whisk the All-Purpose Breading, cornmeal, Cajun Seasoning, and salt until blended. In a second shallow bowl, whisk together the eggs and hot sauce.
2. One at a time, dip the oysters in the cornmeal mixture, the eggs, and again in the cornmeal, coating thoroughly.
3. Preheat the air fryer to 400°F. Line the air fryer tray with parchment paper.
4. Place the oysters on the parchment and spritz with oil.
5. Cook for 2 minutes. Shake the basket, spritz the oysters with oil, and cook for 3 minutes more until lightly browned and crispy.
6. Spread each sandwich half with Pecan Tartar Sauce. Assemble the po'boys by layering each sandwich with fried oysters, ½ cup shredded lettuce, and 2 tomato slices.

◆ **Shrimp Po'boy:** Replace the oysters with 1 pound fresh or frozen peeled, deveined shrimp with tails removed. Proceed with the recipe as directed.

Per Serving (1 sandwich): Calories: 648; Total fat: 38g; Saturated fat: 8g; Cholesterol: 113mg; Sodium: 1,546mg; Carbohydrates: 59g; Fiber: 4.5g; Protein: 15g

TROUT AMANDINE WITH LEMON BUTTER SAUCE

TRUE CLASSIC

Serves: 4 · **Prep:** 20 minutes · **Fry time:** 8 minutes

Amandine, also almondine, is a garnish of almonds. Here, almonds become a delicious, nutty, cheesy crust. Be sure the almonds are finely crushed—almost to a powder.

FOR THE TROUT AMANDINE

⅔ cup almonds, toasted

⅓ cup grated Parmesan cheese

1 teaspoon salt

½ teaspoon freshly ground black pepper

2 tablespoons butter, melted

4 (4-ounce) trout fillets, or salmon fillets

1 to 2 tablespoons oil

FOR THE LEMON BUTTER SAUCE

8 tablespoons (1 stick) butter, melted

2 tablespoons freshly squeezed
   lemon juice

½ teaspoon Worcestershire sauce

½ teaspoon salt

½ teaspoon freshly ground black pepper

¼ teaspoon hot sauce

TO MAKE THE TROUT AMANDINE

1. In a blender or food processor, pulse the almonds for 5 to 10 seconds until finely processed. Transfer to a shallow bowl and whisk in the Parmesan cheese, salt, and pepper. Place the melted butter in another shallow bowl.
2. One at a time, dip the fish in the melted butter, then the almond mixture, coating thoroughly.
3. Preheat the air fryer to 300°F. Line the air fryer tray with parchment paper.
4. Place the coated fish on the parchment and spritz with oil.
5. Cook for 4 minutes. Flip the fish, spritz it with oil, and cook for 4 minutes more until the fish flakes easily with a fork.

Continued ❯

TO MAKE THE LEMON BUTTER SAUCE

6. In a small bowl, whisk the butter, lemon juice, Worcestershire sauce, salt, pepper, and hot sauce until blended.

7. Serve with the fish.

◆ **Southern Know-How:** To toast almonds, preheat the air fryer to 350° F. Line the air fryer tray with parchment paper. Spread the almonds on the parchment and spritz with oil. Cook for 3 minutes. Shake the basket; cook for 2 minutes more until lightly browned.

Per Serving: Calories: 615; Total fat: 53g; Saturated fat: 22g; Cholesterol: 147mg; Sodium: 1,177mg; Carbohydrates: 6g; Fiber: 2.5g; Protein: 30g

CRAWFISH CREOLE CASSEROLE

FAMILY FAVORITE

Serves: 4 · **Prep:** 20 minutes · **Fry time:** 25 minutes

When you think of Louisiana you might think crawfish, but did you know Louisiana produces almost one-third of all seafood eaten in America? The state is also the nation's top producer of oysters, farming more than 120 million pounds during a good year.

1½ cups crawfish meat

½ cup chopped celery

½ cup chopped onion

½ cup chopped green bell pepper

2 large eggs, beaten

1 cup half-and-half

1 tablespoon butter, melted

1 tablespoon cornstarch

1 teaspoon Creole Seasoning (page 16)

¾ teaspoon salt

½ teaspoon freshly ground black pepper

1 cup shredded Cheddar cheese

1 to 2 tablespoons oil

1. In a medium bowl, stir together the crawfish, celery, onion, and green pepper.
2. In another medium bowl, whisk the eggs, half-and-half, butter, cornstarch, Creole Seasoning, salt, and pepper until blended. Stir the egg mixture into the crawfish mixture. Add the cheese and stir to combine.
3. Preheat the air fryer to 300°F. Spritz a 6-inch air fryer–safe pan with oil.
4. Transfer the crawfish mixture to the prepared pan and place it on the air fryer tray.
5. Cook for 25 minutes, stirring every 10 minutes, until a knife inserted into the center comes out clean.

◆ **Crab Creole Casserole:** If crawfish aren't available in your area, substitute 1½ cups crabmeat or imitation crabmeat.

Per Serving: Calories: 383; Total fat: 25g; Saturated fat: 13g; Cholesterol: 271mg; Sodium: 872mg; Carbohydrates: 9g; Fiber: 1g; Protein: 29g

FRIED CATFISH WITH DIJON SAUCE

NEW TRADITION

Serves: 4 • **Prep:** 20 minutes • **Fry time:** 7 to 10 minutes

Did you know three cities lay claim to the title "Catfish Capital of the World?" They are Savannah, Tennessee (with their catfish statue), Belzoni, Mississippi (with their World Catfish Festival held each April), and Des Allemands, Louisiana (which hosts the annual Louisiana Catfish Festival in June). You'll love this version (pictured on page 58).

4 tablespoons butter, melted

2 teaspoons Worcestershire sauce, divided

1 teaspoon lemon pepper

1 cup panko bread crumbs

4 (4-ounce) catfish fillets

1 to 2 tablespoons oil

½ cup sour cream

1 tablespoon Dijon mustard

1. In a shallow bowl, stir together the melted butter, 1 teaspoon of Worcestershire sauce, and the lemon pepper. Place the bread crumbs in another shallow bowl.
2. One at a time, dip both sides of the fillets in the butter mixture, then the bread crumbs, coating thoroughly.
3. Preheat the air fryer to 300°F. Line the air fryer tray with parchment paper.
4. Place the coated fish on the parchment and spritz with oil.
5. Cook for 4 minutes. Flip the fish, spritz it with oil, and cook for 3 to 6 minutes more, depending on the thickness of the fillets, until the fish flakes easily with a fork.
6. In a small bowl, stir together the sour cream, Dijon, and remaining 1 teaspoon of Worcestershire sauce. This sauce can be made 1 day in advance and refrigerated before serving. Serve with the fried fish.

◆ **Southern Know-How:** When choosing fish fillets, select pieces that are not discolored or dry, which are signs the fish is not fresh. Water collecting in the bottom of the package means the fish is losing moisture.

Per Serving: Calories: 357; Total fat: 23g; Saturated fat: 9.5g; Cholesterol: 99mg; Sodium: 806mg; Carbohydrates: 16g; Fiber: 0g; Protein: 19g

CAJUN FISH FILLETS

TRUE CLASSIC

Serves: 4 · **Prep:** 15 minutes · **Fry time:** 6 to 8 minutes

Although there are 3,000 species of catfish in the world, only 39 can be found in North America. Of these, 12 are native to the South. The largest catfish caught in the Mississippi River was found near Alton, Illinois—124 pounds and 58 inches long.

¾ cup All-Purpose Breading (page 18)

¼ cup yellow cornmeal

1 large egg, beaten

¼ cup Cajun Seasoning (page 16)

4 (4-ounce) catfish fillets

1 to 2 tablespoons oil

Pecan Tartar Sauce (page 21)

1. In a shallow bowl, whisk the All-Purpose Breading and cornmeal until blended. Place the egg in a second shallow bowl and the Cajun Seasoning in a third shallow bowl.
2. One at a time, dip the catfish fillets in the breading, the egg, and the Cajun Seasoning, coating thoroughly.
3. Preheat the air fryer to 300°F. Line the air fryer tray with parchment paper.
4. Place the coated fish on the parchment and spritz with oil.
5. Cook for 3 minutes. Flip the fish, spritz it with oil, and cook for 3 to 5 minutes more until the fish flakes easily with a fork and reaches an internal temperature of 145°F. Serve with the Pecan Tartar Sauce.

◆ **Southern Know-How:** The catfish can also be chopped into small, 1-inch pieces and fried as nuggets, just like chicken.

Per Serving: Calories: 554; Total fat: 42g; Saturated fat: 9g; Cholesterol: 121mg; Sodium: 1,527mg; Carbohydrates: 22g; Fiber: 2.5g; Protein: 22g

NEW ORLEANS–STYLE CRAB CAKES

FAMILY FAVORITE

Serves: 4 • **Prep:** 20 minutes • **Fry time:** 8 to 10 minutes

Pam has been a fan of crab cakes since the first bite she tasted as a child. When her aunt gifted her a vintage Creole cookbook from the 1950s, she adapted its crab cake recipe to suit her family's tastes. This was the result.

1¼ cups bread crumbs

2 teaspoons Creole Seasoning (page 16)

1 teaspoon dry mustard

1 teaspoon salt

1 teaspoon freshly ground black pepper

1½ cups crabmeat

2 large eggs, beaten

1 teaspoon butter, melted

⅓ cup minced onion

1 to 2 tablespoons oil

Pecan Tartar Sauce (page 21)

1. In a medium bowl, whisk the bread crumbs, Creole Seasoning, dry mustard, salt, and pepper until blended. Add the crabmeat, eggs, butter, and onion. Stir until blended. Shape the crab mixture into 8 patties.
2. Preheat the air fryer to 350°F. Line the air fryer tray with parchment paper.
3. Place the crab cakes on the parchment and spritz with oil.
4. Cook for 4 minutes. Flip the cakes, spritz them with oil, and cook for 4 to 6 minutes more until the outsides are firm and a fork inserted into the center comes out clean. Serve with the Pecan Tartar Sauce.

◆ **Shrimp Cakes:** Substitute 1 pound cooked, peeled shrimp with tails removed for the crabmeat. In a food processor or blender, pulse the shrimp for about 5 seconds until finely chopped. Mix with the eggs, melted butter, and onion.

Per Serving (2 crab cakes): Calories: 578; Total fat: 39g; Saturated fat: 8.5g; Cholesterol: 217mg; Sodium: 1,630mg; Carbohydrates: 31g; Fiber: 2.5g; Protein: 24g

FINGER-LICKIN' CHICKEN

BAKED APRICOT CHICKEN

FAMILY FAVORITE

Serves: 4 · **Prep:** 15 minutes · **Fry time:** 10 to 12 minutes

Gainesville, Georgia, claims to be the "poultry capital of the world." To commemorate this achievement, they've installed a monument with a life-size bird on top. According to a 1961 ordinance issued as a publicity stunt, it is illegal to eat chicken with a fork in Gainesville.

⅔ cup apricot preserves

2 tablespoons freshly squeezed
   lemon juice

1 teaspoon soy sauce

¼ teaspoon salt

¾ cup panko bread crumbs

2 whole boneless, skinless chicken breasts
   (1 pound each), halved

1 to 2 tablespoons oil

1. In a shallow bowl, stir together the apricot preserves, lemon juice, soy sauce, and salt. Place the bread crumbs in a second shallow bowl.
2. Roll the chicken in the preserves mixture and then the bread crumbs, coating thoroughly.
3. Preheat the air fryer to 350°F. Line the air fryer tray with parchment paper.
4. Place the coated chicken on the parchment and spritz with oil.
5. Cook for 5 minutes. Flip the chicken, spritz it with oil, and cook for 5 to 7 minutes more until the internal temperature reaches 165°F and the chicken is no longer pink inside. Let sit for 5 minutes.

♦ **Variation:** Substitute ⅔ cup peach preserves or orange marmalade for the apricot preserves.

Per Serving: Calories: 412; Total fat: 9g; Saturated fat: 2g; Cholesterol: 125mg; Sodium: 489mg; Carbohydrates: 33g; Fiber: 0g; Protein: 47g

CRISPY DILL CHICKEN STRIPS

NEW TRADITION

Serves: 4 • **Prep:** 15 minutes, plus 1 hour to marinate • **Fry time:** 10 minutes

These crunchy chicken strips are a kid's favorite. Save the crumbs and small pieces from bags of chips and store them in the freezer. You'll always have chips on hand for this recipe. Create new taste combinations by mixing different flavors of chips.

---

2 whole boneless, skinless chicken breasts (about 1 pound each), halved lengthwise

1 cup Italian dressing

3 cups finely crushed potato chips

1 tablespoon dried dill weed

1 tablespoon garlic powder

1 large egg, beaten

1 to 2 tablespoons oil

1. In a large resealable bag, combine the chicken and Italian dressing. Seal the bag and refrigerate to marinate at least 1 hour.
2. In a shallow dish, stir together the potato chips, dill, and garlic powder. Place the beaten egg in a second shallow dish.
3. Remove the chicken from the marinade. Roll the chicken pieces in the egg and the potato chip mixture, coating thoroughly.
4. Preheat the air fryer to 325°F. Line the air fryer tray with parchment paper.
5. Place the coated chicken on the parchment and spritz with oil.
6. Cook for 5 minutes. Flip the chicken, spritz it with oil, and cook for 5 minutes more until the outsides are crispy and the insides are no longer pink.

◆ **Southern Know-How:** For a perfectly tender piece of chicken, soak the chicken in buttermilk before cooking for at least 1 hour, or overnight, before soaking in the Italian dressing. Don't have buttermilk on hand? Make a substitute by combining 8 ounces whole milk with 1 tablespoon freshly squeezed lemon juice. Let sit 10 minutes before using it.

Per Serving: Calories: 637; Total fat: 32g; Saturated fat: 5.5g; Cholesterol: 156mg; Sodium: 544mg; Carbohydrates: 32g; Fiber: 2g; Protein: 51g

PECAN-CRUSTED CHICKEN

NEW TRADITION

Serves: 4 • **Prep:** 15 minutes • **Fry time:** 10 to 12 minutes

Almost everyone thinks pecans are nuts, but they are actually "drupes," a fruit consid-ered to be a close relative of peaches and plums. The trees only produce nuts every two years, but the pecans add a delicious crunch to these chicken strips.

¾ cup chopped toasted pecans

½ cup panko bread crumbs

1 teaspoon dried rosemary leaves, crushed

½ teaspoon salt

½ teaspoon dried sage

¼ teaspoon dried basil

⅛ teaspoon cayenne pepper

1 large egg, beaten

2 whole boneless, skinless chicken breasts (about 1 pound each), halved

1 to 2 tablespoons oil

1. In a blender or food processor, process the pecans for 5 to 10 seconds, or until finely ground. Add the bread crumbs, rosemary, salt, sage, basil, and cayenne. Process for 3 seconds. Transfer to a shallow bowl. Place the beaten egg in a second shallow bowl.
2. Roll the chicken pieces in the beaten egg and the pecan mixture, coating thoroughly.
3. Preheat the air fryer to 350°F. Line the air fryer tray with parchment paper.
4. Place the coated chicken on the parchment and spritz with oil.
5. Cook for 8 minutes. Flip the chicken, spritz it with oil, and cook for 2 to 4 minutes more until the crust is flaky and the chicken is no longer pink inside.

♦ **Variations:** For a Creole version, omit the rosemary, sage, and basil. Substitute 2 tea-spoons Creole Seasoning (page 16). For a dill and garlic variation, omit the rosemary, sage, and basil. Substitute 1 teaspoon dried dill weed and 1 teaspoon garlic powder.

Per Serving: Calories: 412; Total fat: 20g; Saturated fat: 3g; Cholesterol: 156mg; Sodium: 458mg; Carbohydrates: 9g; Fiber: 1.5g; Protein: 49g

POTATO-CRUSTED CHICKEN

NEW TRADITION

Serves: 4 · **Prep:** 15 minutes · **Fry time:** 22 to 25 minutes

When Brittany was diagnosed with celiac disease, she missed the platters of crispy chicken she once enjoyed. This was our compromise. Our potato-crusted chicken recipe is naturally gluten-free and tastes as juicy and crispy as the real thing.

¼ cup buttermilk

1 large egg, beaten

1 cup instant potato flakes

¼ cup grated Parmesan cheese

1 teaspoon salt

½ teaspoon freshly ground black pepper

2 whole boneless, skinless chicken breasts
  (about 1 pound each), halved

1 to 2 tablespoons oil

1. In a shallow bowl, whisk the buttermilk and egg until blended. In another shallow bowl, stir together the potato flakes, cheese, salt, and pepper.
2. One at a time, dip the chicken pieces in the buttermilk mixture and the potato flake mixture, coating thoroughly.
3. Preheat the air fryer to 400°F. Line the air fryer tray with parchment paper.
4. Place the coated chicken on the parchment and spritz with oil.
5. Cook for 15 minutes. Flip the chicken, spritz it with oil, and cook for 7 to 10 minutes more until the outside is crispy and the inside is no longer pink.

♦ **Southern Know-How:** Keep fresh chicken in the coldest part of the refrigerator for no more than 2 days. If not using within that time, it can be frozen for up to 9 months. Wrap pieces in aluminum foil before freezing them in an airtight, freezer-safe container to prevent freezer burn.

Per Serving: Calories: 344; Total fat: 11g; Saturated fat: 3g; Cholesterol: 176mg; Sodium: 595mg; Carbohydrates: 8g; Fiber: 0.5g; Protein: 49g

CLASSIC FRIED CHICKEN

TRUE CLASSIC

Serves: 4 · **Prep:** 15 minutes · **Fry time:** 20 minutes

This is a slight adaptation of fried chicken recipes (pictured on page 72) from both Pam's mom and her mother-in-law. For a thicker coating, roll the chicken in the flour, then the eggs, and again in the flour, before dipping in the panko.

1 cup all-purpose flour

1 teaspoon salt

1 teaspoon freshly ground black pepper

1 teaspoon paprika

1 large egg, beaten

1 cup panko bread crumbs

2 whole boneless, skinless chicken breasts (about 1 pound each), halved

1 to 2 tablespoons oil

1. In a shallow bowl, whisk the flour, salt, pepper, and paprika until blended. Place the beaten egg in a second shallow bowl and the bread crumbs in a third shallow bowl.
2. One at a time, dip the chicken pieces in the flour mixture, the beaten egg, and the bread crumbs, coating thoroughly.
3. Preheat the air fryer to 400°F. Line the air fryer tray with parchment paper.
4. Place the coated chicken on the parchment and spritz with oil.
5. Cook for 10 minutes. Flip the chicken, spritz it with oil, and cook for 10 minutes more until the outside is crispy and the inside is no longer pink.

♦ **Spice It Up:** Make garlic-ginger chicken. Reduce the paprika to ½ teaspoon. Add 1 teaspoon garlic powder, 1 teaspoon ground ginger, and 1 teaspoon ground coriander to the flour mixture.

Per Serving: Calories: 433; Total fat: 11g; Saturated fat: 2.5g; Cholesterol: 172mg; Sodium: 808mg; Carbohydrates: 29g; Fiber: 0.5g; Protein: 51g

GARLIC CHICKEN WINGS

NEW TRADITION

Serves: 4 · **Prep:** 15 minutes · **Fry time:** 16 to 18 minutes

You're sure to attract family and guests to the kitchen when the smell of these wings wafts through the house. Tender on the inside, crisp on the outside, this dish will be a hit at any tailgate.

1¼ cups grated Parmesan cheese
1 tablespoon garlic powder
1 teaspoon salt
½ teaspoon freshly ground black pepper

¾ cup all-purpose flour
1 large egg, beaten
12 chicken wings (about 1 pound)
1 to 2 tablespoons oil

1. In a shallow bowl, whisk the Parmesan cheese, garlic powder, salt, and pepper until blended. Place the flour in a second shallow bowl and the beaten egg in a third shallow bowl.
2. One at a time, dip the chicken wings into the flour, the beaten egg, and the Parmesan cheese mixture, coating thoroughly.
3. Preheat the air fryer to 390°F. Line the air fryer tray with parchment paper.
4. Place the chicken wings on the parchment and spritz with oil.
5. Cook for 8 minutes. Flip the chicken, spritz it with oil, and cook for 8 to 10 minutes more until the internal temperature reaches 165° F and the insides are no longer pink. Let sit for 5 minutes before serving.

◆ **Southern Know-How:** No grated Parmesan? Make your own. Cut a wedge of Parmesan into 1-inch cubes and place them in a blender or food processor. Process until the cheese reaches your desired texture. Refrigerate leftover grated cheese in an airtight bag.

Per Serving (3 wings): Calories: 309; Total fat: 18g; Saturated fat: 6g; Cholesterol: 136mg; Sodium: 751mg; Carbohydrates: 14g; Fiber: 0.5g; Protein: 21g

BLACKENED CHICKEN

NEW TRADITION

Serves: 4 · **Prep:** 10 minutes · **Fry time:** 20 minutes

Blackening was invented by Louisiana chef Paul Prudhomme. He developed this recipe by seasoning fish in his special spice blend and then cooking it in a very hot skillet. We owe him our thanks for popularizing delicious Cajun cooking methods.

1 large egg, beaten
¾ cup Blackened Seasoning (page 17)

2 whole boneless, skinless chicken breasts
    (about 1 pound each), halved
1 to 2 tablespoons oil

1. Place the beaten egg in one shallow bowl and the Blackened Seasoning in another shallow bowl.
2. One at a time, dip the chicken pieces in the beaten egg and the Blackened Seasoning, coating thoroughly.
3. Preheat the air fryer to 360°F. Line the air fryer tray with parchment paper.
4. Place the chicken pieces on the parchment and spritz with oil.
5. Cook for 10 minutes. Flip the chicken, spritz it with oil, and cook for 10 minutes more until the internal temperature reaches 165°F and the chicken is no longer pink inside. Let sit for 5 minutes before serving.

♦ **Southern Know-How:** Substitute bone-in chicken thighs for boneless chicken breasts. These take longer to cook but are economical and don't dry out as easily as chicken breasts. Leave the skin on during cooking for extra crispiness.

Per Serving: Calories: 307; Total fat: 11g; Saturated fat: 2.5g; Cholesterol: 172mg; Sodium: 1,293mg; Carbohydrates: 3g; Fiber: 1g; Protein: 48g

SPICY FRIED CHICKEN BREAST

NEW TRADITION

Serves: 4 • **Prep:** 15 minutes • **Fry time:** 12 minutes

The crushed cheese crackers give this dish an extra flavor punch. For a spicier version, substitute zesty, spicy, or pepper Jack cheese crackers. This chicken is delicious served with a buffalo dipping sauce, a creamy ranch dip, or Peachy Barbecue Sauce (page 20).

¾ cup all-purpose flour

¼ cup yellow cornmeal

2 tablespoons Creole Seasoning (page 16)

2 tablespoons onion powder

2 tablespoons garlic powder

1 tablespoon paprika

1 teaspoon cayenne pepper

1 large egg, beaten

1 cup finely crushed cheese crackers

2 whole boneless, skinless chicken breasts (about 1 pound each), halved

1 to 2 tablespoons oil

1. In a shallow bowl, whisk the flour, cornmeal, Creole Seasoning, onion powder, garlic powder, paprika, and cayenne until blended. Place the beaten egg in a second shallow bowl and the crushed crackers to a third shallow bowl.
2. One at a time, dip the chicken pieces in the flour mixture, the egg mixture, and the crushed cheese crackers, coating thoroughly.
3. Preheat the air fryer to 400° F. Line the air fryer tray with parchment paper.
4. Place the coated chicken on the parchment and spritz with oil.
5. Cook for 6 minutes. Flip the chicken, spritz it with oil, and cook for 6 minutes more until the coating is crispy.

♦ **Southern Know-How:** Many recipes call for meat to be "dredged" in flour. This simply means coating both sides of the meat with flour before cooking. Dredging adds extra flavor to food and gives the meat a tasty browned crust.

Per Serving: Calories: 457; Total fat: 14g; Saturated fat: 3.5g; Cholesterol: 172mg; Sodium: 677mg; Carbohydrates: 28g; Fiber: 1.5g; Protein: 51g

HONEY-ROSEMARY CHICKEN

FAMILY FAVORITE

Serves: 4 · **Prep:** 10 minutes, plus 2 hours to marinate · **Fry time:** 20 minutes

Did you know vinegar has been used for more than 7,000 years? Its history can be traced back to ancient Babylonia where it was used in food preparation and for medicinal purposes. Stored in a cool, dry place, vinegar should last for years.

¼ cup balsamic vinegar

¼ cup honey

2 tablespoons olive oil

1 tablespoon dried rosemary leaves

1 teaspoon salt

½ teaspoon freshly ground black pepper

2 whole boneless, skinless chicken breasts (about 1 pound each), halved

1 to 2 tablespoons oil

1. In a large resealable bag, combine the vinegar, honey, olive oil, rosemary, salt, and pepper. Add the chicken pieces, seal the bag, and refrigerate to marinate for at least 2 hours.
2. Preheat the air fryer to 325°F. Line the air fryer tray with parchment paper.
3. Remove the chicken from the marinade and place it on the parchment. Spritz with oil.
4. Cook for 10 minutes. Flip the chicken, spritz it with oil, and cook for 10 minutes more until the internal temperature reaches 165° F and the chicken is no longer pink inside. Let sit for 5 minutes before serving.

◆ **Spice It Up:** Omit the rosemary. Add 1 teaspoon Italian-Style Seasoning (page 17), 1 teaspoon garlic powder, and 1 tablespoon light brown sugar to the marinade.

Per Serving: Calories: 307; Total fat: 10g; Saturated fat: 2g; Cholesterol: 125mg; Sodium: 494mg; Carbohydrates: 5g; Fiber: 0g; Protein: 46g

BACON-WRAPPED CHICKEN BREAST

FAMILY FAVORITE

Serves: 4 • **Prep:** 15 minutes • **Fry time:** 20 minutes

Did you know bacon arrived in the Americas in 1493 when the first pigs arrived with Columbus? Pork became so popular that, in 1708, poet Ebenezer Cook wrote The Sot-Weed Factor *complaining about the amount of bacon used in colonists' dishes.*

---

2 teaspoons onion powder

2 teaspoons garlic powder

2 teaspoons paprika

1 teaspoon salt

1 teaspoon freshly ground black pepper

2 whole boneless, skinless chicken breasts
   (about 1 pound each), halved

4 thin-sliced deli ham pieces

4 uncooked bacon slices

1 to 2 tablespoons oil

1. In a small bowl, whisk the onion powder, garlic powder, paprika, salt, and pepper until blended. Evenly sprinkle the mixture over the chicken pieces. Place 1 ham slice on each piece of chicken.
2. Preheat the air fryer to 400°F. Line the air fryer tray with parchment paper.
3. Place the chicken on the parchment and spritz with oil.
4. Cook for 10 minutes.
5. Wrap 1 bacon slice around each piece of chicken and ham. Flip the chicken pieces and return the tray to the air fryer. Cook for 10 minutes more until the internal temperature reaches 165°F and the chicken is no longer pink inside. Let sit for 5 minutes before serving.

◆ **Southern Know-How:** Bacon can be frozen for up to 2 months. Separate the slices, placing 4 on a piece of parchment. Continue with the remaining bacon. Layer the bacon and parchment paper in an airtight freezer bag. This technique works well for packaging single servings.

Per Serving: Calories: 321; Total fat: 12g; Saturated fat: 3g; Cholesterol: 138mg; Sodium: 978mg; Carbohydrates: 0g; Fiber: 0g; Protein: 50g

CHAPTER EIGHT

~

PRIZED PORK

BACON-WRAPPED PORK TENDERLOIN

TRUE CLASSIC

Serves: 6 • **Prep:** 10 minutes, plus 2 hours to marinate • **Fry time:** 22 to 25 minutes

Did you know the term "Uncle Sam" began with pork? During the War of 1812, a meat packer named Uncle Sam Wilson sent a few hundred barrels of pork stamped with "U.S." to the soldiers. The rest, as they say, is history.

½ cup minced onion

½ cup hard apple cider, or apple juice

¼ cup honey

1 tablespoon minced garlic

¼ teaspoon salt

¼ teaspoon freshly ground black pepper

2 pounds pork tenderloin

1 to 2 tablespoons oil

8 uncooked bacon slices

1. In a medium bowl, stir together the onion, hard cider, honey, garlic, salt, and pepper. Transfer to a large resealable bag or airtight container and add the pork. Seal the bag. Refrigerate to marinate for at least 2 hours.
2. Preheat the air fryer to 400°F. Line the air fryer tray with parchment paper.
3. Remove the pork from the marinade and place it on the parchment. Spritz with oil.
4. Cook for 15 minutes.
5. Wrap the bacon slices around the pork and secure them with toothpicks. Turn the pork roast and spritz with oil. Cook for 7 to 10 minutes more until the internal temperature reaches 145°F, depending on how well-done you like pork loin. It will continue cooking after it's removed from the fryer, so let it sit for 5 minutes before serving.

♦ **Spice It Up:** Omit the hard cider. Add ½ cup white wine or ½ cup craft beer, 2 teaspoons Creole Seasoning (page 16), and 2 tablespoons light brown sugar.

Per Serving: Calories: 300; Total fat: 15g; Saturated fat: 4.5g; Cholesterol: 112mg; Sodium: 313mg; Carbohydrates: 3g; Fiber: 0g; Protein: 36g

HAM HOCK MAC 'N' CHEESE

FAMILY FAVORITE

Serves: 4 · **Prep:** 20 minutes · **Fry time:** 25 minutes

Pam got this recipe from her mother-in-law, who had added a handwritten note beside the recipe saying, "Brittany thinks best." Pam uses ham hocks to give it classic Southern flair. If you don't have ham hocks, substitute ½ cup diced cooked ham and increase the salt to 1 teaspoon.

---

2 large eggs, beaten

2 cups cottage cheese, whole milk or 2%

2 cups grated sharp Cheddar
cheese, divided

1 cup sour cream

½ teaspoon salt

1 teaspoon freshly ground black pepper

2 cups uncooked elbow macaroni

2 ham hocks (about 11 ounces each), meat
removed and diced

1 to 2 tablespoons oil

1. In a large bowl, stir together the eggs, cottage cheese, 1 cup of the Cheddar cheese, sour cream, salt, and pepper.
2. Stir in the macaroni and the diced meat.
3. Preheat the air fryer to 360°F. Spritz an 8-inch air fryer–safe pan with oil.
4. Pour the macaroni mixture into the prepared pan, making sure all noodles are covered with sauce.
5. Cook for 12 minutes. Stir in the remaining 1 cup of Cheddar cheese, making sure all the noodles are covered with sauce. Cook for 13 minutes more, until the noodles are tender. Let rest for 5 minutes before serving.

◆ **Spice It Up:** Mix ¾ cup panko bread crumbs with 1 teaspoon Creole Seasoning (page 16) or Cajun Seasoning (page 16). Cook the macaroni and cheese as directed for 12 minutes. Sprinkle on the bread crumb mixture and finish the recipe as instructed.

Per Serving: Calories: 729; Total fat: 40g; Saturated fat: 20g; Cholesterol: 218mg; Sodium: 1,451mg; Carbohydrates: 46g; Fiber: 2g; Protein: 44g

BLACKENED CAJUN PORK ROAST

TRUE CLASSIC

Serves: 4 • **Prep:** 20 minutes • **Fry time:** 33 minutes

Many people think Cajun recipes have to be hot and spicy. That's not always the case. Most Cajun dishes start with "the holy trinity"—equal parts onion, celery, and green bell pepper. This is good served with Two-Cheese Grits (page 28).

2 pounds bone-in pork loin roast

2 tablespoons oil

¼ cup Cajun Seasoning (page 16)

½ cup diced onion

½ cup diced celery

½ cup diced green bell pepper

1 tablespoon minced garlic

1. Cut 5 slits across the pork roast. Spritz it with oil, coating it completely. Evenly sprinkle the Cajun Seasoning over the pork roast.
2. In a medium bowl, stir together the onion, celery, green bell pepper, and garlic until combined. Set aside.
3. Preheat the air fryer to 360°F. Line the air fryer with parchment paper.
4. Place the pork roast on the parchment and spritz with oil.
5. Cook for 5 minutes. Flip the roast and cook for 5 minutes more. Continue to flip and cook in 5-minute increments for a total cook time of 20 minutes.
6. Increase the air fryer temperature to 390°F.
7. Cook the roast for 8 minutes more and flip. Add the vegetable mixture to the tray and cook for a final 5 minutes. Let the roast sit for 5 minutes before serving.

◆ **Southern Know-How:** Although pork tenderloin and pork roast look similar, a pork roast is bigger and needs a longer cook time. When shopping, look for roasts with a pinkish-red color. Avoid pale meat or meat with dark spots.

Per Serving: Calories: 415; Total fat: 26g; Saturated fat: 8g; Cholesterol: 102mg; Sodium: 1,297mg; Carbohydrates: 7g; Fiber: 2g; Protein: 37g

FRUITED HAM

FAMILY FAVORITE

Serves: 4 · **Prep:** 15 minutes · **Fry time:** 8 to 10 minutes

Cuts of pork go well with many fruits, especially apricots, peaches, cherries, pineapple, strawberries, apples, and cranberries. Experiment with one fruit or a variety. Pair the fruit with a complementary fruit jam, jelly, or preserves to create a blend you like.

---

1 cup orange marmalade

¼ cup packed light brown sugar

¼ teaspoon ground cloves

½ teaspoon dry mustard

1 to 2 tablespoons oil

1 pound cooked ham, cut into 1-inch cubes

½ cup canned mandarin oranges, drained and chopped

1. In a small bowl, stir together the orange marmalade, brown sugar, cloves, and dry mustard until blended. Set aside.
2. Preheat the air fryer to 320°F. Spritz a 6-inch air fryer–safe pan with oil.
3. Place the ham cubes in the prepared pan. Pour the marmalade sauce over the ham to glaze it.
4. Cook for 4 minutes. Stir and cook for 2 minutes more.
5. Add the mandarin oranges and cook for 2 to 4 minutes more until the sauce begins to thicken and the ham is tender.

♦ **Variations:** For a pineapple twist, add ½ cup drained pineapple tidbits to the marmalade mix. You can also try swapping apricot preserves for the orange marmalade. For something peachy, swap 1 cup peach preserves and ½ cup finely chopped canned peaches for the orange marmalade.

Per Serving: Calories: 408; Total fat: 8.5g; Saturated fat: 2.5g; Cholesterol: 50mg; Sodium: 1,530mg; Carbohydrates: 73g; Fiber: 1g; Protein: 16g

PORK CHOPS WITH CARAMELIZED ONIONS AND PEPPERS

FAMILY FAVORITE

Serves: 4 • **Prep:** 20 minutes • **Fry time:** 23 to 34 minutes

While these peppers and onions aren't caramelized in the traditional way (they're normally sautéed), this dish is still packed with flavor. Serve it with Cheesy Corn Bread (page 42), Corn Custard (page 54), and Peach Crumble (page 124).

---

4 bone-in pork chops (8 ounces each)

1 to 2 tablespoons oil

2 tablespoons Cajun Seasoning (page 16), divided

1 yellow onion, thinly sliced

1 green bell pepper, thinly sliced

2 tablespoons light brown sugar

1. Spritz the pork chops with oil. Sprinkle 1 tablespoon of Cajun Seasoning on one side of the chops.
2. Preheat the air fryer to 400°F. Line the air fryer tray with parchment paper and spritz the parchment with oil.
3. Place 2 pork chops, spice-side up, on the paper.
4. Cook for 4 minutes. Flip the chops, sprinkle with the remaining 1 tablespoon of Cajun Seasoning, and cook for 4 to 8 minutes more until the internal temperature reaches 145°F, depending on the chops' thickness. Remove and keep warm while you cook the remaining 2 chops. Set the chops aside.
5. In an 8-inch air fryer–safe pan, combine the onion, bell pepper, and brown sugar, stirring until the vegetables are coated. Place the pan on the air fryer tray and cook for 4 minutes.
6. Stir the vegetables. Cook for 3 to 6 minutes more to your desired doneness. Spoon the vegetable mixture over the chops to serve.

♦ **Southern Know-How:** Refrigerate fresh cuts of pork for 2 to 4 days. To freeze pork, place it into an airtight freezer bag and use it within 6 months.

Per Serving: Calories: 300; Total fat: 15g; Saturated fat: 3g; Cholesterol: 90mg; Sodium: 673mg; Carbohydrates: 12g; Fiber: 1.5g; Protein: 29g

SMOTHERED CHOPS

TRUE CLASSIC

Serves: 4 · **Prep:** 20 minutes · **Fry time:** 30 minutes

"Smothering" usually involves cooking foods in liquid over low heat for a long time. Our version speeds up the process by making the sauce separately.

---

4 bone-in pork chops (8 ounces each)

2 teaspoons salt, divided

1½ teaspoons freshly ground black pepper, divided

1 teaspoon garlic powder

1 cup tomato puree

1½ teaspoons Italian-Style Seasoning (page 17)

1 tablespoon sugar

1 tablespoon cornstarch

½ cup chopped onion

½ cup chopped green bell pepper

1 to 2 tablespoons oil

1. Evenly season the pork chops with 1 teaspoon salt, 1 teaspoon pepper, and the garlic powder.
2. In a medium bowl, stir together the tomato puree, Italian-Style Seasoning, sugar, remaining 1 teaspoon of salt, and remaining ½ teaspoon of pepper.
3. In a small bowl, whisk ¾ cup water and the cornstarch until blended. Stir this slurry into the tomato puree, with the onion and green bell pepper. Transfer to a 6-inch air fryer–safe pan.
4. Preheat the air fryer to 350°F.
5. Place the sauce in the fryer and cook for 10 minutes. Stir and cook for 10 minutes more. Remove the pan and keep warm.
6. Increase the air fryer temperature to 400°F. Line the air fryer tray with parchment paper.
7. Place the pork chops on the parchment and spritz with oil.
8. Cook for 5 minutes. Flip and spritz the chops with oil and cook for 5 minutes more, until the internal temperature reaches 145°F. Serve with the tomato mixture spooned on top.

◆ **Spice It Up:** Rub the chops with oil and season with 2 tablespoons of Creole (page 16), Cajun (page 16), or Blackened (page 17) Seasoning. Add ½ cup celery to the bell pepper mixture.

Per Serving: Calories: 306; Total fat: 14g; Saturated fat: 3g; Cholesterol: 89mg; Sodium: 1,377mg; Carbohydrates: 14g; Fiber: 2g; Protein: 30g

COUNTRY-FRIED RIB CHOPS

NEW TRADITION

Serves: 4 • **Prep:** 15 minutes • **Fry time:** 10 to 12 minutes

These country-fried chops also have a crunchy cheese crust, making them flavorful enough to serve without the traditional brown gravy. Serve them with Drop Biscuits (page 24), Fried Green Tomatoes and Dipping Sauce (page 38), and a big glass of sweet tea.

⅔ cup All-Purpose Breading (page 18)

¼ cup grated Parmesan cheese

2 large eggs, beaten

1½ cups crushed cheese crackers

4 rib chops (6 ounces each)

1 to 2 tablespoons oil

1. In a shallow bowl, stir together the All-Purpose Breading and Parmesan cheese. Place the beaten eggs in a second shallow bowl and the crushed crackers in a third shallow bowl.
2. One at a time, dip the rib chops in the breading, the egg, and the cheese crackers, coating thoroughly.
3. Preheat the air fryer to 400°F. Line the air fryer tray with parchment paper.
4. Place the rib chops on the parchment and spritz with oil.
5. Cook for 5 minutes. Flip the chops, spritz them with oil, and cook for 5 to 7 minutes more, until the internal temperature reaches 145°F.

◆ **Spice It Up:** Add 2 tablespoons Cajun Seasoning (page 16) to the breading in step 1.

Per Serving: Calories: 409; Total fat: 22g; Saturated fat: 6.5g; Cholesterol: 106mg; Sodium: 471mg; Carbohydrates: 24g; Fiber: 1g; Protein: 27g

BARBECUE CHOPS

FAMILY FAVORITE

Serves: 4 • **Prep:** 15 minutes • **Fry time:** 10 to 12 minutes

Take a trip to South Carolina and you'll probably find a "famous" mustard sauce at every barbecue joint. The thick sauce is flavored with mustard, spices, and the tang of vinegar. We use dry mustard in our version, but you can substitute 3 tablespoons prepared mustard, if you wish.

½ cup ketchup

2 tablespoons distilled white vinegar

2 tablespoons light brown sugar

1½ teaspoons salt

1½ teaspoons dry mustard

½ teaspoon chili powder

4 bone-in pork chops (8 ounces each)

1 to 2 tablespoons oil

1. In a medium bowl, whisk 1 cup water, the ketchup, vinegar, brown sugar, salt, dry mustard, and chili powder until blended.
2. Preheat the air fryer to 400°F. Line the air fryer tray with parchment paper and spritz it with oil.
3. Place the chops on the parchment and baste with the ketchup mixture.
4. Cook for 4 minutes. Flip the chops, spritz them with oil, baste again, and cook for 6 to 8 minutes more until the internal temperature reaches 145°F, depending on their thickness. Serve with any extra sauce.

♦ **Alabama Barbecue Chops:** To make a white sauce, omit the ketchup, water, and chili powder. Add 1 cup mayonnaise, 1 tablespoon freshly squeezed lemon juice, ½ teaspoon cayenne pepper, 1 teaspoon hot sauce, 1 teaspoon garlic powder, and increase the vinegar to ¼ cup.

Per Serving: Calories: 316; Total fat: 14g; Saturated fat: 3g; Cholesterol: 89mg; Sodium: 1,281mg; Carbohydrates: 17g; Fiber: 0g; Protein: 28g

BARBECUE PULLED PORK SANDWICHES

TRUE CLASSIC

Serves: 4 · **Prep:** 15 minutes · **Fry time:** 30 minutes

Did you know the term "barbecue" was coined by French pirates who sailed to the Caribbean? The word comes from de barbe à queue, *which means "from head to tail," as the entire pig could be used for food. If you like, layer these sandwiches (pictured on page 84) with pickles and coleslaw.*

1½ cups prepared barbecue sauce

2 tablespoons distilled white vinegar

2 tablespoons light brown sugar

1 tablespoon minced garlic

1 teaspoon hot sauce

2 pounds pork shoulder roast

1 to 2 tablespoons oil

4 sandwich buns

1. In a medium bowl, stir together the barbecue sauce, vinegar, brown sugar, garlic, and hot sauce.
2. Preheat the air fryer to 360°F. Line the air fryer tray with parchment paper and spritz it with oil.
3. Place the pork on the parchment and baste it with a thick layer of sauce.
4. Cook for 5 minutes. Flip the pork and baste with sauce. Repeat 3 more times for a total of 20 minutes of cook time, ending with basting.
5. Increase the air fryer temperature to 390°F.
6. Cook the pork for 5 minutes. Flip and baste. Cook for 5 minutes more. Flip and baste. Let sit for 5 minutes before pulling the pork into 1-inch pieces. Transfer to a bowl and toss the pork with the remaining sauce. Serve on buns.

◆ **Variations:** For a creative twist on the sauce, omit the vinegar and garlic. Add ¼ cup pineapple juice and 1 teaspoon honey for something sweet. Or make a cola version by adding ¼ cup soda to the sauce as is.

Per Serving (1 sandwich): Calories: 736; Total fat: 29g; Saturated fat: 9.5g; Cholesterol: 137mg; Sodium: 1,389mg; Carbohydrates: 71g; Fiber: 4g; Protein: 40g

HAM WITH SWEET POTATOES

NEW TRADITION

Serves: 4 • **Prep:** 20 minutes • **Fry time:** 15 to 17 minutes

Mississippi is the nation's second largest producer of sweet potatoes, led by only North Carolina. To celebrate their long history with this crop, each year, the small town of Vardaman, Mississippi, holds their annual Sweet Potato Festival. Along with crowning a Sweet Potato Queen, participants sample all sorts of sweet potato dishes, including sweet potato fudge.

1 cup freshly squeezed orange juice

½ cup packed light brown sugar

1 tablespoon Dijon mustard

½ teaspoon salt

½ teaspoon freshly ground black pepper

3 sweet potatoes, cut into small wedges

2 ham steaks (8 ounces each), halved

1 to 2 tablespoons oil

1. In a large bowl, whisk the orange juice, brown sugar, Dijon, salt, and pepper until blended. Toss the sweet potato wedges with the brown sugar mixture.
2. Preheat the air fryer to 400°F. Line the air fryer tray with parchment paper and spritz with oil.
3. Place the sweet potato wedges on the parchment.
4. Cook for 10 minutes.
5. Place ham steaks on top of the sweet potatoes and brush everything with more of the orange juice mixture.
6. Cook for 3 minutes. Flip the ham and cook or 2 to 4 minutes more until the sweet potatoes are soft and the glaze has thickened. Cut the ham steaks in half to serve.

◆ **Spice It Up:** Add some apple wedges to the sweet potato wedges for a riff on a classic pork roast.

Per Serving: Calories: 388; Total fat: 8.5g; Saturated fat: 2g; Cholesterol: 51mg; Sodium: 1,882mg; Carbohydrates: 53g; Fiber: 3g; Protein: 24g

HONEY-BAKED PORK LOIN

FAMILY FAVORITE

Serves: 6 • **Prep:** 10 minutes, plus 2 hours to marinate • **Fry time:** 22 to 25 minutes

Pork has long been a staple on the Southern dinner table. Southerners found that pigs were low-maintenance animals that could be allowed to roam freely. Before refrigeration, the meat could be preserved and stored for a long time by curing it with salt or smoke.

¼ cup honey

¼ cup freshly squeezed lemon juice

2 tablespoons soy sauce

1 teaspoon garlic powder

1 (2-pound) pork loin

2 tablespoons vegetable oil

1. In a medium bowl, whisk together the honey, lemon juice, soy sauce, and garlic powder. Reserve half of the mixture for basting during cooking.
2. Cut 5 slits in the pork loin and transfer it to a resealable bag. Add the remaining honey mixture. Seal the bag and refrigerate to marinate for at least 2 hours.
3. Preheat the air fryer to 400°F. Line the air fryer tray with parchment paper.
4. Remove the pork from the marinade, and place it on the parchment. Spritz with oil, then baste with the reserved marinade.
5. Cook for 15 minutes. Flip the pork, baste with more marinade and spritz with oil again. Cook for 7 to 10 minutes more until the internal temperature reaches 145°F. Let rest for 5 minutes before serving.

♦ **Southern Know-How:** If you want the leanest cut of pork, choose one that has "loin" in the name. Pork loin is extremely lean, with 16 percent less fat than it had 20 years ago, and 75 percent less fat than in 1950. While cooking, check frequently to prevent overcooking.

Per Serving: Calories: 289; Total fat: 16g; Saturated fat: 4.5g; Cholesterol: 82mg; Sodium: 459mg; Carbohydrates: 9g; Fiber: 0g; Protein: 29g

BARBECUE COUNTRY-STYLE BONELESS RIBS

NEW TRADITION

Serves: 4 • **Prep:** 10 minutes, plus 8 hours to marinate • **Fry time:** 15 minutes

The secret to the sauce for this dish is cola. Not only does the acid in the cola tenderize the meat, but it also adds a distinctly sweet flavor. Pair these ribs with Deviled Eggs (page 43) and Peach Crumble (page 124) for a summer feast.

2 cups cola

3 tablespoons light brown sugar

2 teaspoons garlic powder

2 teaspoons paprika

2 teaspoons Italian-Style Seasoning (page 17)

1 teaspoon salt

½ teaspoon freshly ground black pepper

2 pounds boneless pork ribs

2 cups Peachy Barbecue Sauce (page 20)

1. In a medium bowl, stir together the cola, brown sugar, garlic powder, paprika, Italian-Style Seasoning, salt, and pepper. Reserve ½ cup of the cola mixture for basting during cooking.
2. In a large resealable plastic bag, combine the remaining cola mixture and the ribs. Seal the bag and refrigerate to marinate for 8 hours. Remove the ribs from the cola mixture.
3. Preheat the air fryer to 350°F. Line the air fryer tray with parchment paper.
4. Place the ribs on the parchment and brush with the reserved cola mixture.
5. Cook for 6 minutes. Flip the ribs and baste with the cola mixture. Cook for 7 to 9 minutes more until the internal temperature reaches 145°F. Let sit for 2 to 3 minutes before serving with the Peachy Barbecue Sauce.

♦ **Spice It Up:** Omit the spices and barbecue sauce. Mix the brown sugar with 2 tablespoons Creole Seasoning (page 16) or Blackened Seasoning (page 17) and coat the ribs.

Per Serving (3 ribs): Calories: 831; Total fat: 37g; Saturated fat: 13g; Cholesterol: 143mg; Sodium: 1,171mg; Carbohydrates: 85g; Fiber: 0g; Protein: 39g

CHAPTER NINE

~

BEST IN BEEF

PEPPER STEAK

TRUE CLASSIC

Serves: 4 · **Prep:** 15 minutes, plus 8 hours to marinate · **Fry time:** 16 to 20 minutes

Pam adapted this recipe from a battered version of the 1961 cookbook Favorite Recipes of American Home Economics Teachers: Meats, *a gift from her aunt. This is good served over rice or noodles, or with a side of mashed potatoes.*

---

1 pound cube steak, cut into 1-inch pieces

1 cup Italian dressing

1½ cups beef broth

1 tablespoon soy sauce

½ teaspoon salt

¼ teaspoon freshly ground black pepper

¼ cup cornstarch

1 cup thinly sliced bell pepper, any color

1 cup chopped celery

1 tablespoon minced garlic

1 to 2 tablespoons oil

1. In a large resealable bag, combine the beef and Italian dressing. Seal the bag and refrigerate to marinate for 8 hours.
2. In a small bowl, whisk the beef broth, soy sauce, salt, and pepper until blended.
3. In another small bowl, whisk ¼ cup water and the cornstarch until dissolved. Stir the cornstarch mixture into the beef broth mixture until blended.
4. Preheat the air fryer to 375°F.
5. Pour the broth mixture into a 6-inch air fryer–safe pan. Cook for 4 minutes. Stir and cook for 4 to 5 minutes more. Remove and set aside.
6. Increase the air fryer temperature to 400°F. Line the air fryer tray with parchment paper.
7. Remove the steak from the marinade and place it in a medium bowl. Discard the marinade. Stir in the bell pepper, celery, and garlic.

8. Place the steak and pepper mixture on the parchment. Spritz with oil.

9. Cook for 4 minutes. Shake the basket and cook for 4 to 7 minutes more, until the vegetables are tender and the meat reaches an internal temperature of 145°F. Serve with the gravy.

♦ **Southern Know-How:** Patting the steak dry before seasoning helps the seasonings or coatings adhere better.

Per Serving: Calories: 274; Total fat: 12g; Saturated fat: 3g; Cholesterol: 69mg; Sodium: 1,292mg; Carbohydrates: 13g; Fiber: 1g; Protein: 27g

CHICKEN-FRIED STEAK

FAMILY FAVORITE

Serves: 4 · **Prep:** 20 minutes · **Fry time:** 20 minutes

The origins of chicken-fried steak are murky. Some food historians claim a version of the dish was found in Southern cookbooks as early as the 1800s. Pig Stand restaurant, a Texas chain, claims to be the first to serve the chicken-fried steak sandwich. No matter who discovered it, it's delicious.

4 cube steaks (5 ounces each)

1 teaspoon salt

1 teaspoon freshly ground black pepper

2 large eggs, beaten

1½ cups Bread Crumb Coating (page 18)

1 to 2 tablespoons oil

1. Evenly season the steaks all over with salt and pepper.
2. Place the beaten eggs in a shallow bowl and the Bread Crumb Coating in a second shallow bowl.
3. One at a time, dip each steak into the egg and then the breading mixture, coating thoroughly.
4. Preheat the air fryer to 350°F. Line the air fryer tray with parchment paper.
5. Place 2 steaks on the parchment and spritz with oil.
6. Cook for 5 minutes. Turn the steaks and spritz both sides with oil. Cook for 5 minutes more until browned and crispy. Repeat with the remaining 2 steaks.

♦ **Spice It Up:** Add 1 tablespoon Creole Seasoning (page 16) to the Bread Crumb Coating (page 18); or use 1 cup Nashville Hot Breading (page 18) plus an additional 1 teaspoon chili powder; or add 1 teaspoon Italian-Style Seasoning (page 17) to the All-Purpose Breading (page 18).

Per Serving: Calories: 339; Total fat: 14g; Saturated fat: 4.5g; Cholesterol: 138mg; Sodium: 1,435mg; Carbohydrates: 14g; Fiber: 0.5g; Protein: 37g

SOUTHERN CHILI

TRUE CLASSIC

Serves: 4 • **Prep:** 20 minutes • **Fry time:** 25 minutes

"Southern" chili is sweeter than other chilis, not too spicy, and includes onion and bell pepper. This recipe makes a very thick chili, which is delicious over noodles and topped with additional minced onion and Cheddar cheese. If you prefer, omit the garlic powder and add 1 tablespoon minced garlic to the ground beef and onion mixture before cooking.

1 pound ground beef (85% lean)

1 cup minced onion

1 (28-ounce) can tomato puree

1 (15-ounce) can diced tomatoes with green chilies

1 (15-ounce) can light red kidney beans, rinsed and drained

¼ cup Chili Seasoning (page 17)

1. Preheat the air fryer to 400°F.
2. In a 9-inch air fryer–safe pan, mix the ground beef and onion. Place the pan in the air fryer.
3. Cook for 4 minutes. Stir and cook for 4 minutes more until browned. Remove the pan from the fryer. Drain the meat and transfer to a large bowl.
4. Reduce the air fryer temperature to 350°F.
5. To the bowl with the meat, add in the tomato puree, diced tomatoes and green chilies, kidney beans, and Chili Seasoning. Mix well. Pour the mixture into an 8- or 9-inch air fryer–safe pan. The dish will be full.
6. Cook for 25 minutes, stirring every 10 minutes, until thickened.

♦ **Variation:** When the chili is finished cooking, stir in 1 cup sour cream.

Per Serving: Calories: 425; Total fat: 13g; Saturated fat: 4.5g; Cholesterol: 71mg; Sodium: 2,880mg; Carbohydrates: 47g; Fiber: 13g; Protein: 32g

TANGY MEATBALLS

NEW TRADITION

Serves: 6 • **Prep:** 20 minutes • **Fry time:** 20 minutes

These meatballs are delicious served as appetizers, used in spaghetti, or added to egg noodles with a creamy gravy. If you can't find a bottle of chili sauce (I like the one Heinz makes), see the tip below for creating your own.

1½ pounds ground beef (85% lean)
2¼ cups crushed cheese crackers
1 large egg, beaten
½ cup chili sauce
½ cup minced onion

1 tablespoon minced garlic
1 teaspoon salt
1 teaspoon freshly ground black pepper
1 to 2 tablespoons oil
Peachy Barbecue Sauce (page 20)

1. In a large bowl, mix the ground beef, crushed cheese crackers, egg, chili sauce, onion, garlic, salt, and pepper until blended. Shape the mixture into 30 (1-inch) meatballs.
2. Preheat the air fryer to 350°F. Line the air fryer tray with parchment paper.
3. Place half the meatballs on the parchment and spritz with oil.
4. Cook for 5 minutes. Shake the basket and cook for 5 minutes more, until the meatballs are browned. Set the meatballs aside and keep warm. Repeat with the remaining meatballs.
5. Serve with the Peachy Barbecue Sauce.

◆ **Southern Know-How:** Make your own chili sauce: Mix 1 cup ketchup, 2 tablespoons light brown sugar, 2 tablespoons distilled white vinegar, ½ teaspoon chili powder, 1 teaspoon garlic powder, 1 teaspoon onion powder, 1 teaspoon Worcestershire sauce, and 1 tablespoon freshly squeezed lemon juice.

Per Serving (6 meatballs + sauce): Calories: 660; Total fat: 24g; Saturated fat: 7.5g; Cholesterol: 107mg; Sodium: 1,167mg; Carbohydrates: 83g; Fiber: 1g; Protein: 28g

PEACHY BARBECUE MEAT LOAF

NEW TRADITION

Serves: 6 · **Prep:** 30 minutes · **Fry time:** 45 minutes

Georgia is nicknamed the Peach State, but South Carolina produces three times the number of peaches. If you're in the mood for peach cobbler, visit the annual Georgia Peach Festival in Fort Valley. Each year they make the world's largest peach cobbler, measuring 11 feet by 5 feet.

1½ pounds ground beef (85% lean)

1 cup panko bread crumbs

½ cup minced onion

½ cup minced bell pepper, any color

½ cup finely chopped mushrooms

1 teaspoon salt

1 large egg

1½ cups Peachy Barbecue Sauce (page 20), divided

1 to 2 tablespoons oil

1. In a large bowl, mix the ground beef, bread crumbs, onion, bell pepper, mushrooms, and salt until blended.
2. Add the egg and 1 cup of Peachy Barbecue Sauce. Mix to combine.
3. Preheat the air fryer to 375°F.
4. Spritz an 8-inch air fryer–safe pan with cooking oil. Add the meat mixture to the pan. Cover the pan with aluminum foil and place it on the air fryer tray.
5. Cook for 40 minutes. Uncover the meat loaf. Spread the remaining ½ cup Peachy Barbecue Sauce over the meat loaf. Cook for 5 minutes more until the glaze has thickened and the meat is no longer pink on the inside.

♦ **Peachy Barbecue Meatballs:** Mix the ingredients per steps 1 and 2. Shape into about 30 (1-inch) meatballs and roll them in 1 cup crushed panko bread crumbs. Working in batches, cook at 350°F for 4 minutes, shake the basket, and cook for 4 minutes more. Serve with Peachy Barbecue Sauce.

Per Serving: Calories: 469; Total fat: 19g; Saturated fat: 7.5g; Cholesterol: 101mg; Sodium: 1,035mg; Carbohydrates: 50g; Fiber: 0.5g; Protein: 25g

CUBE STEAK ROLL-UPS

FAMILY FAVORITE

Serves: 4 · **Prep:** 10 minutes, plus 2 hours to marinate · **Fry time:** 8 to 10 minutes

These steak roll-ups are brimming with tender vegetables. You can adjust the amount of vegetables to suit your family's taste or substitute red, yellow, or orange bell peppers for color. Serve with a side of rice, quinoa, new potatoes, green beans, or corn on the cob.

---

4 cube steaks (6 ounces each)

1 (16-ounce) bottle Italian dressing

1 teaspoon salt

½ teaspoon freshly ground black pepper

½ cup finely chopped yellow onion

½ cup finely chopped green bell pepper

½ cup finely chopped mushrooms

1 to 2 tablespoons oil

1. In a large resealable bag or airtight storage container, combine the steaks and Italian dressing. Seal the bag and refrigerate to marinate for 2 hours.
2. Remove the steaks from the marinade and place them on a cutting board. Discard the marinade. Evenly season the steaks with salt and pepper.
3. In a small bowl, stir together the onion, bell pepper, and mushrooms. Sprinkle the onion mixture evenly over the steaks. Roll up the steaks, jelly roll–style, and secure with toothpicks.
4. Preheat the air fryer to 400°F.
5. Place the steaks on the air fryer tray.
6. Cook for 4 minutes. Flip the steaks and spritz them with oil. Cook for 4 to 6 minutes more until the internal temperature reaches 145°F. Let rest for 5 minutes before serving.

◆ **Herby Steak Roll-Ups:** Omit the mushrooms. Add ¼ cup finely minced celery and 1 teaspoon minced garlic.

Per Serving: Calories: 346; Total fat: 18g; Saturated fat: 4.5g; Cholesterol: 103mg; Sodium: 1,359mg; Carbohydrates: 6g; Fiber: 0.5g; Protein: 38g

BEEF WHIRLS

NEW TRADITION

Serves: 6 · **Prep:** 5 minutes, plus 2 hours to marinate · **Fry time:** 18 minutes

Cube steak is sometimes referred to as minute steak in some parts of the United States and Canada because of its quick cooking time. This cut of beef is usually tenderized and cut from top round or top sirloin. Cube steaks are often used for chicken-fried steak, but these juicy beef whirls give them an entirely new flavor.

3 cube steaks (6 ounces each)
1 (16-ounce) bottle Italian dressing
1 cup Italian-style bread crumbs
½ cup grated Parmesan cheese
1 teaspoon dried basil

1 teaspoon dried oregano
1 teaspoon dried parsley
¼ cup beef broth
1 to 2 tablespoons oil

1. In a large resealable bag, combine the steaks and Italian dressing. Seal the bag and refrigerate to marinate for 2 hours.
2. In a medium bowl, whisk the bread crumbs, cheese, basil, oregano, and parsley until blended. Stir in the beef broth.
3. Place the steaks on a cutting board and cut each in half so you have 6 equal pieces. Sprinkle with the bread crumb mixture. Roll up the steaks, jelly roll–style, and secure with toothpicks.
4. Preheat the air fryer to 400°F.
5. Place 3 roll-ups on the air fryer tray.
6. Cook for 5 minutes. Flip the roll-ups and spritz with oil. Cook for 4 minutes more until the internal temperature reaches 145°F. Repeat with the remaining roll-ups. Let rest for 5 to 10 minutes before serving.

◆ **Spice It Up:** Omit the basil, oregano, and parsley. Add 1 tablespoon Blackened Seasoning (page 17) to the bread crumbs.

Per Serving: Calories: 285; Total fat: 14g; Saturated fat: 3.5g; Cholesterol: 57mg; Sodium: 859mg; Carbohydrates: 16g; Fiber: 0.5g; Protein: 23g

"PORCUPINE" MEATBALLS

TRUE CLASSIC

Serves: 4 · **Prep:** 10 minutes · **Fry time:** 32–34 minutes

The first time Pam served these meatballs to her children, they refused to eat them because they did not want to eat porcupines. "Where do you even find porcupine?" they asked. She had to explain that the porcupine quill-like rice gave them their name. Serve with Peachy Barbecue Sauce (page 20), if you like.

---

1 cup instant rice

2 teaspoons salt, divided

1 tablespoon butter

1 pound ground beef (85% lean)

½ cup finely chopped onion

½ cup finely chopped green bell pepper

2 teaspoons garlic powder

1 teaspoon freshly ground black pepper

1 to 2 tablespoons oil

1. Preheat the air fryer to 350°F. Meanwhile, mix 1 cup instant rice, 1 cup water, 1 teaspoon salt, and butter in an air fryer–safe pan. Cook the rice for 6 minutes. Stir and cook for 6 to 8 minutes more until done.
2. In a large bowl, mix the ground beef, cooked rice, onion, green bell pepper, garlic powder, the remaining 1 teaspoon of salt, and pepper. Shape the mixture into 20 (1-inch) meatballs.
3. Line the air fryer tray with parchment paper. Place 10 meatballs on the parchment.
4. Cook for 5 minutes. Shake the basket and spritz the meatballs with oil. Cook for 5 minutes more until browned and firm. Remove the meatballs and keep warm. Repeat with the remaining meatballs.

♦ **Creole Meatballs:** Add ½ cup finely chopped celery and 1 teaspoon Creole Seasoning (page 16) to the mixture in step 2.

Per Serving (5 meatballs): Calories: 684; Total fat: 20g; Saturated fat: 6.5g; Cholesterol: 80mg; Sodium: 1,252mg; Carbohydrates: 96g; Fiber: 3g; Protein: 29g

SOUTHERN-STYLE COLA MEAT LOAF

FAMILY FAVORITE

Serves: 6 • **Prep:** 20 minutes • **Fry time:** 45 minutes

Coca-Cola is often thought to have originated in Georgia, but the first Coke was bottled in Vicksburg, Mississippi. Visitors can tour the Biedenharn Coca-Cola Museum there and purchase a Coke float at their restored soda-fountain counter. If you can't find a bottle of chili sauce (I like the one Heinz makes), see Southern Know-How at the bottom of the recipe for creating your own.

FOR THE GLAZE
¾ cup chili sauce
½ cup cola
1 tablespoon mustard
1 tablespoon cornstarch

FOR THE MEAT LOAF
1½ cups panko bread crumbs
1½ teaspoons Italian-Style Seasoning
    (page 17)

1 teaspoon salt
½ teaspoon freshly ground black pepper
1½ pounds ground beef (85% lean)
½ cup minced onion
1 large egg
¾ cup chili sauce
½ cup cola
2 tablespoons ketchup
1½ tablespoons mustard
1 to 2 tablespoons oil

TO MAKE THE GLAZE
1. In a small bowl, whisk the chili sauce, cola, mustard, and cornstarch until blended.
2. Set aside, covered.

TO MAKE THE MEAT LOAF
3. In a large bowl, whisk the bread crumbs, Italian-Style Seasoning, salt, and pepper. Add the ground beef, onion, egg, chili sauce, cola, ketchup, and mustard. Mix until blended.
4. Preheat the air fryer to 375°F. Spritz an 8-inch air fryer–safe pan with oil.

Continued ❯

5. Add the meat loaf mixture to the prepared pan. Cover with aluminum foil and place on the air fryer tray.
6. Cook for 20 minutes. Uncover the meat loaf. Whisk the glaze and spread it over the meat loaf. Recover and cook for 25 minutes, more until the glaze has thickened and the meat loaf is no longer pink inside.

◆ **Southern Know-How:** To make your own chili sauce, mix 1 cup ketchup, 2 tablespoons light brown sugar, 2 tablespoons distilled white vinegar, ½ teaspoon chili powder, 1 teaspoon garlic powder, 1 teaspoon onion powder, 1 teaspoon Worcestershire sauce, and 1 tablespoon freshly squeezed lemon juice.

Per Serving: Calories: 490; Total fat: 21g; Saturated fat: 7.5g; Cholesterol: 102mg; Sodium: 1,939mg; Carbohydrates: 49g; Fiber: 0.5g; Protein: 25g

HAMBURGER STEAK WITH MUSHROOM GRAVY

FAMILY FAVORITE

Serves: 4 • **Prep:** 20 minutes • **Fry time:** 29 to 34 minutes

This classic dish (pictured on page 98) saves time with an easy shortcut gravy made from onion soup mix. If you like, add 10 thin onion slices to the gravy before cooking. Serve the steak with leftover mashed potatoes or buttered noodles for a truly comforting meal.

FOR THE MUSHROOM GRAVY

1 (1-ounce) envelope dry onion soup mix

⅓ cup cornstarch

1 cup diced mushrooms

FOR THE HAMBURGER STEAK

1 pound ground beef (85% lean)

¾ cup minced onion

½ cup Italian-style bread crumbs

2 teaspoons Worcestershire sauce

1 teaspoon salt

1 teaspoon freshly ground black pepper

1 to 2 tablespoons oil

TO MAKE THE MUSHROOM GRAVY

1. In a 6-inch air fryer–safe bowl, whisk the soup mix, cornstarch, mushrooms, and 2 cups water until blended.
2. Preheat the air fryer to 350°F.
3. Place the bowl on the air fryer tray.
4. Cook for 10 minutes. Stir and cook for 5 to 10 minutes more to your desired thickness.

TO MAKE THE HAMBURGER STEAK

5. In a large bowl, mix the ground beef, onion, bread crumbs, Worcestershire sauce, salt, and pepper until blended. Shape the beef mixture into 4 patties.
6. Decrease the air fryer's temperature to 320°F.

Continued ❯

7. Place the patties on the air fryer tray.
8. Cook for 7 minutes. Flip the patties, spritz them with oil, and cook for 7 minutes more, until the internal temperature reaches 145°F.

♦ **Southern Know-How:** Ground beef can be kept refrigerated for 1 to 2 days before cooking, or frozen for 3 to 4 months. Ground beef can also be cooked and frozen in an airtight container for up to 3 months.

Per Serving (1 patty + gravy): Calories: 377; Total fat: 18g; Saturated fat: 5.5g; Cholesterol: 75mg; Sodium: 1,264mg; Carbohydrates: 28g; Fiber: 2g; Protein: 25g

CHAPTER TEN

~

RIGHT QUICK DESSERTS

APPLE FRITTERS

TRUE CLASSIC

Serves: 6 · **Prep:** 30 minutes · **Fry time:** 7 to 8 minutes

Apple fritters have been around for centuries. The first published recipe for an apple fritter may date back to England, in 1390, under the name "Frytor of Pastronakes of Skyrwypts and Apples." Of course, you can find them in most any bakery in the South today.

1 cup chopped peeled Granny Smith apple
½ cup granulated sugar
1 teaspoon ground cinnamon
1 cup all-purpose flour
1 teaspoon baking powder
1 teaspoon salt

1 large egg, beaten
2 tablespoons milk
2 tablespoons butter, melted
1 to 2 tablespoons oil
¼ cup confectioners' sugar (optional)

1. In a small bowl, combine the apple, granulated sugar, and cinnamon. Let sit for 30 minutes.
2. In a medium bowl, whisk the flour, baking powder, and salt until blended. Stir in the egg, milk, and melted butter to combine.
3. Add the apple mixture to the flour mixture and stir to combine. Shape the fritter dough into 12 (1-inch) balls.
4. Preheat the air fryer to 350°F. Line the air fryer tray with parchment paper and spritz it with oil.
5. Place the fritters on the parchment and spritz with oil.
6. Cook for 4 minutes. Shake the tray and spritz the fritters with oil. Cook for 3 to 4 minutes more until lightly browned.
7. Sprinkle the warm fritters with confectioners' sugar (if using).

◆ **Variations:** Omit the apples and substitute either 1 cup chopped fresh pear or 1 cup chopped frozen peaches and add ½ teaspoon almond extract.

Per Serving (2 fritters): Calories: 222; Total fat: 7.5g; Saturated fat: 3g; Cholesterol: 42mg; Sodium: 403mg; Carbohydrates: 36g; Fiber: 1.5g; Protein: 3g

PEACH FRIED PIES

TRUE CLASSIC

Makes: 8 pies · **Prep:** 15 minutes · **Fry time:** 20 minutes

Light, flaky handheld fried pies (pictured on page 114) are the perfect summer dessert. Filled with apples, peaches, pears, or a mix of fruit, they're delicious when served with a tall glass of sweet tea. Use canned pie filling to save time.

1 (14.75-ounce) can sliced peaches in heavy syrup
1 teaspoon ground cinnamon
1 tablespoon cornstarch

1 large egg
All-purpose flour, for dusting
2 refrigerated piecrusts

1. Reserving 2 tablespoons of syrup, drain the peaches well. Chop the peaches into bite-size pieces, transfer to a medium bowl, and stir in the cinnamon.
2. In a small bowl, stir together the reserved peach juice and cornstarch until dissolved. Stir this slurry into the peaches.
3. In another small bowl, beat the egg.
4. Dust a cutting board or work surface with flour and spread the piecrusts on the prepared surface. Using a knife, cut each crust into 4 squares (8 squares total).
5. Place 2 tablespoons of peaches onto each dough square. Fold the dough in half and seal the edges. Using a pastry brush, spread the beaten egg on both sides of each hand pie. Using a knife, make 2 thin slits in the top of each pie.
6. Preheat the air fryer to 350°F.
7. Line the air fryer tray with parchment paper. Place 4 pies on the parchment.
8. Cook for 10 minutes. Flip the pies, brush with beaten egg, and cook for 5 minutes more. Repeat with the remaining pies.

♦ **Variations:** Omit the peaches. Substitute 1 cup diced apple and ½ teaspoon ground cinnamon or use ⅔ cup store-bought lemon pie filling.

Per Serving (1 pie): Calories: 285; Total fat: 14g; Saturated fat: 5.5g; Cholesterol: 34mg; Sodium: 294mg; Carbohydrates: 42g; Fiber: 1g; Protein: 3g

KENTUCKY CHOCOLATE NUT PIE

FAMILY FAVORITE

Serves: 8 · **Prep:** 20 minutes · **Fry time:** 25 minutes

Did you know the term "derby pie," in reference to that famously sweet nutty choco-latey pie associated with the Kentucky Derby, is copyrighted? The only licensed maker of "Derby-Pie" is Kern's Kitchen in Louisville, Kentucky. To make it at home, put on your derby hat and try our copycat chocolate nut version—just don't call it derby pie.

---

2 large eggs, beaten

⅓ cup butter, melted

1 cup sugar

½ cup all-purpose flour

1½ cups coarsely chopped pecans

1 cup milk chocolate chips

2 tablespoons bourbon

1 (9-inch) unbaked piecrust

1. In a large bowl, stir together the eggs and melted butter. Add the sugar and flour and stir until combined. Stir in the pecans, chocolate chips, and bourbon until well mixed.
2. Using a fork, prick holes in the bottom and sides of the pie crust. Pour the pie filling into the crust.
3. Preheat the air fryer to 350°F.
4. Cook for 25 minutes, or until a knife inserted into the middle of the pie comes out clean. Let set for 5 minutes before serving.

◆ **Southern Know-How:** Pecans have a higher fat content than other types of nuts, which makes them more perishable. Keep shelled pecans fresh for up to 6 months by storing them in the freezer instead of the pantry.

Per Serving: Calories: 583; Total fat: 36g; Saturated fat: 13g; Cholesterol: 77mg; Sodium: 176mg; Carbohydrates: 60g; Fiber: 3g; Protein: 7g

MAPLE BACON MOONSHINE BREAD PUDDING

NEW TRADITION

Serves: 6 · **Prep:** 20 minutes · **Fry time:** 15 minutes

When Pam was a child, her father made homemade cough syrup using moonshine purchased from a family member who had a hidden still in the woods. Picking a few leaves out of the moonshine was common. These days, you can buy flavored moonshine from the store—leaves optional. This is delicious served with whipped cream or ice cream.

1 cup whole milk

1 (4.6-ounce) package cook-and-serve vanilla pudding and pie filling

¼ cup granulated sugar

2 large eggs, beaten

1 tablespoon butter, melted

1 teaspoon ground cinnamon

1 teaspoon vanilla extract

4 cups loosely packed cubed French bread

¼ cup packed light brown sugar

½ cup chopped toasted pecans

¾ cup maple bacon moonshine, plus 3 tablespoons

1 to 2 tablespoons oil

1. In a large bowl, whisk the milk, pudding mix, granulated sugar, eggs, melted butter, cinnamon, and vanilla until blended. Add the bread cubes and let soak for 10 minutes.
2. In a small bowl, stir together the brown sugar, pecans, and ¾ cup moonshine. Stir the pecan mixture into the bread mixture.
3. Preheat the air fryer to 355°F. Spritz an 8-by-8-inch air fryer–safe pan with oil.
4. Transfer the bread mixture to the prepared pan.
5. Bake for 10 minutes. The bottom of the pudding will still be mushy. Stir. Bake for 5 minutes more and stir again. The pudding will be soft, but not runny, and a knife inserted into the middle will have soft crumbs attached.
6. Drizzle the remaining 3 tablespoons of maple bacon moonshine over the pudding.

◆ **Variation:** Substitute golden rum or bourbon for the maple bacon moonshine.

Per Serving: Calories: 439; Total fat: 14g; Saturated fat: 3.5g; Cholesterol: 71mg; Sodium: 292mg; Carbohydrates: 52g; Fiber: 1.5g; Protein: 6g

FRIED CANDIED APPLES

NEW TRADITION

Serves: 4 • **Prep:** 15 minutes • **Fry time:** 12 minutes

Georgia produces 22 varieties of apples during their growing season, from late July until December. When choosing fresh apples, look for firm apples with no bruising or discoloration and an enticing aroma. These apples are our version of the fried apples you find at Cracker Barrel restaurants.

---

1 cup packed light brown sugar

2 teaspoons ground cinnamon

2 medium Granny Smith apples, peeled and diced

1. In a medium bowl, stir together the brown sugar and cinnamon. Toss the apples into the mixture and stir to coat. Place the apples in a 6-inch air fryer–safe pan.
2. Preheat the air fryer to 350°F.
3. Place the filled pan on the air fryer tray.
4. Cook for 9 minutes. Stir the apples and cook for 3 minutes more until soft.

◆ **Variation:** Substitute any variety of baking apples, such as Jonathan, Honeycrisp, Golden Delicious, or Red Delicious, for the Granny Smith apples.

Per Serving: Calories: 261; Total fat: 0g; Saturated fat: 0g; Cholesterol: 0mg; Sodium: 16mg; Carbohydrates: 67g; Fiber: 3g; Protein: 0g

BROWN SUGAR BANANA BREAD

NEW TRADITION

Serves: 4 • **Prep:** 20 minutes • **Fry time:** 22 to 24 minutes

This recipe began as a brown sugar doughnut recipe. With a little adaptation, it became a delicious, dense banana bread recipe. Want to take it up a notch? Add ½ cup chopped toasted pecans and another mashed banana to the batter.

1 cup packed light brown sugar

1 large egg, beaten

2 tablespoons butter, melted

½ cup milk, whole or 2%

2 cups all-purpose flour

1½ teaspoons baking powder

1 teaspoon ground cinnamon

½ teaspoon salt

1 banana, mashed

1 to 2 tablespoons oil

¼ cup confectioners' sugar (optional)

1. In a large bowl, stir together the brown sugar, egg, melted butter, and milk.
2. In a medium bowl, whisk the flour, baking powder, cinnamon, and salt until blended. Add the flour mixture to the sugar mixture and stir just to blend.
3. Add the mashed banana and stir to combine.
4. Preheat the air fryer to 350°F. Spritz 2 mini loaf pans with oil.
5. Evenly divide the batter between the prepared pans and place them on the air fryer tray.
6. Cook for 22 to 24 minutes, or until a knife inserted into the middle of the loaves comes out clean.
7. Dust the warm loaves with confectioners' sugar (if using).

♦ **Glazed Banana Bread:** In a medium bowl, stir together 1 cup confectioners' sugar, 1 tablespoon melted butter, ½ teaspoon vanilla extract, and 1 to 2 tablespoons milk until blended. Drizzle the glaze over the bread.

Per Serving: Calories: 591; Total fat: 13g; Saturated fat: 5.5g; Cholesterol: 65mg; Sodium: 339mg; Carbohydrates: 110g; Fiber: 2.5g; Protein: 9g

OLD-FASHIONED FUDGE PIE

TRUE CLASSIC

Serves: 8 · **Prep:** 15 minutes · **Fry time:** 25 to 30 minutes

This classic family recipe was shared by Pam's mother-in-law. Beside the recipe was a handwritten note that said, "Good." What's really good, however, is that pie used to be a popular breakfast food. We don't recommend eating this for breakfast but won't judge if you do. Serve it warm with ice cream or cool with whipped topping.

1½ cups sugar

⅓ cup unsweetened cocoa powder

½ cup self-rising flour

3 large eggs, unbeaten

12 tablespoons (1½ sticks) butter, melted

1½ teaspoons vanilla extract

1 (9-inch) unbaked piecrust

¼ cup confectioners' sugar (optional)

1. In a medium bowl, stir together the sugar, cocoa powder, and flour. Stir in the eggs and melted butter. Stir in the vanilla.
2. Preheat the air fryer to 350°F.
3. Pour the chocolate filing into the crust.
4. Cook for 25 to 30 minutes, stirring every 10 minutes, until a knife inserted into the middle comes out clean. Let sit for 5 minutes before dusting with confectioners' sugar (if using) to serve.

◆ **Southern Know-How:** Don't have self-rising flour? Make your own by mixing 1 cup all-purpose flour, 1½ teaspoons baking powder, and ¼ teaspoon salt until blended. Store the flour in an airtight container.

Per Serving: Calories: 467; Total fat: 26g; Saturated fat: 14g; Cholesterol: 121mg; Sodium: 311mg; Carbohydrates: 59g; Fiber: 1.5g; Protein: 5g

BLACKBERRY COBBLER

FAMILY FAVORITE

Serves: 6 · **Prep:** 15 minutes · **Fry time:** 25 to 30 minutes

Pam's mom would make this in June when fresh blackberries were available. Pam was often recruited to help pick the blackberries, which grew wild on her grandparents' farm. This pie was worth all the thorn pricks and purple-stained fingers she endured.

---

3 cups fresh or frozen blackberries

1¾ cups sugar, divided

1 teaspoon vanilla extract

8 tablespoons (1 stick) butter, melted

1 cup self-rising flour

1 to 2 tablespoons oil

1. In a medium bowl, stir together the blackberries, 1 cup of sugar, and vanilla.
2. In another medium bowl, stir together the melted butter, remaining ¾ cup of sugar, and flour until a dough forms.
3. Spritz a 6-inch air fryer–safe pan with oil. Add the blackberry mixture. Crumble the flour mixture over the fruit. Cover the pan with aluminum foil.
4. Preheat the air fryer to 350°F.
5. Place the covered pan on the air fryer tray. Cook for 20 to 25 minutes until the filling is thickened.
6. Uncover the pan and cook for 5 minutes more, depending on how juicy and browned you like your cobbler. Let sit for 5 minutes before serving.

♦ **Variations:** Omit the blackberries. Substitute any of the following diced fruits: 1½ pints strawberries, apples, cherries, or peaches, or a mixture. Good combinations are 1¼ cups apple and 1¼ cups peaches, or 1¼ cups blackberries and 1¼ cups strawberries.

Per Serving: Calories: 490; Total fat: 18g; Saturated fat: 10g; Cholesterol: 41mg; Sodium: 263mg; Carbohydrates: 81g; Fiber: 4.5g; Protein: 3g

PEACH CRUMBLE

TRUE CLASSIC

Serves: 4 • **Prep:** 45 minutes • **Fry time:** 21 minutes

This was one of the first dishes Pam learned to cook as a child—thanks to her raging sweet tooth. She often substitutes fresh fruit when in season. The warm crumble is delicious served with a scoop of vanilla ice cream or fresh whipped cream.

2 cups frozen diced peaches

½ cup granulated sugar

¼ teaspoon almond extract

1 cup quick-cooking oats

¾ cup packed light brown sugar

½ cup self-rising flour

1 teaspoon ground cinnamon

½ teaspoon salt

8 tablespoons (1 stick) butter, melted

1 to 2 tablespoons oil

1. In a medium bowl, stir together the peaches, granulated sugar, and almond extract. Let sit for 30 minutes.
2. In another medium bowl, stir together the oats, brown sugar, flour, cinnamon, and salt, stirring until blended. Add the melted butter to the oat mixture and stir until coated.
3. Spritz a 6-inch air fryer–safe pan with oil and add the peaches. Top the fruit with the oat mixture. Cover the pan with aluminum foil.
4. Preheat the air fryer to 350°F.
5. Place the covered pan on the air fryer tray.
6. Cook for 15 minutes. Uncover the pan and cook for 6 minutes more until the top is lightly browned and crunchy. Let sit for 5 minutes before serving.

♦ **Variations:** Substitute your favorite diced fruit for the peaches, such as 1 pint apples, strawberries, cherries, or blackberries. If using cherries, strawberries, or blackberries, omit the cinnamon.

Per Serving: Calories: 643; Total fat: 28g; Saturated fat: 15g; Cholesterol: 61mg; Sodium: 501mg; Carbohydrates: 98g; Fiber: 3.5g; Protein: 5g

AIR FRYING TIMES

~

Some nights—or maybe most nights—you might not feel like planning an elaborate meal. That's where our handy cheat sheets come in, well, handy. We've included some of our favorite fresh and frozen foods, along with tips for mixing and matching ingredients with the seasoning blends in chapter 2.

Have a favorite food we haven't included? The rule of thumb when determining cooking time for the air fryer is to reduce the temperature by 25°F and reduce the cooking time by 20 percent.

Want crispier breaded frozen food? Spritz the tray and the top of the food with oil. *Lightly* spritz again when turning the food.

Note: Cooking times can vary among different air fryer models, but these charts give you a starting point. With our tips you'll be able to have dinner on the table before you can say, "Bless your heart."

FRESH FOODS

Fresh Food	Quantity	Time	Temp	Tips	Spice It Up
Bacon	6 to 8 pieces	12 to 15 min	375°F	Turn halfway through the cooking time.	Serve with Bourbon French Toast (page 25).
Broccoli	1 pound	8 to 10 min, depending on desired doneness	400°F	Use florets; toss with 2 tablespoons oil, season with salt and pepper, and place in a steamer bowl; shake halfway through the cooking time.	Toss with Creole Seasoning (page 16).
Brussels sprouts, halved	1 pound	15 to 20 min, depending on desired doneness	380°F	Toss with 2 tablespoons oil and season with salt and pepper; shake the basket halfway through the cooking time.	Toss with Cajun Seasoning (page 16).
Cake	1 (8-inch) cake pan (makes 2 cakes; bake separately)	20 to 25 min	330°F	Spritz cake pan with oil before baking.	Add 1 (3-ounce) package instant pudding to batter.
Carrots	1 pound	15 min	380°F	Place carrots in air fryer tray. Spritz with oil; spritz again and shake halfway through the cooking time.	Toss slices with ¼ cup honey and ½ teaspoon ground nutmeg.
Chicken breast, bone-in	1¼ pounds	25 to 30 min	375°F	Soak in buttermilk for 2 hours; rub chicken with oil and sprinkle with seasonings; turn halfway through the cooking time.	Coat with Cajun Seasoning (page 16) before cooking.
Chicken drumsticks	6	20 to 25 min	370°F	Soak in buttermilk for 2 hours; rub with oil and sprinkle with seasonings; turn halfway through the cooking time.	Coat with Cajun Seasoning (page 16) before cooking.
Chicken thighs, bone-in	6	20 to 22 min	380°F	Soak in buttermilk for 2 hours; rub with oil and sprinkle with seasonings; turn halfway through the cooking time.	Coat with Nashville Hot Breading (page 18) before cooking.
Chickpeas	1 (15.5-ounce) can	15 to 17 min	390°F	Drain; toss with 1 tablespoon oil; shake every 5 minutes while cooking and spritz with oil.	Toss with 1 tablespoon Creole Seasoning (page 16).

Fresh Food	Quantity	Time	Temp	Tips	Spice It Up
Cookies	6 to 8	8 to 10 min	350°F	Line air fryer tray with parchment paper and spritz with oil; shake halfway through the cooking time; let sit for 3 minutes after cooking.	Use vanilla-infused sugar instead of regular sugar in batter.
Cupcakes	9	11 to 12 min	330°F	Use silicone baking cups spritzed with oil.	Add 1 (3-ounce) package instant pudding to batter.
Fish fillets	1 pound	10 min	400°F	Spritz with oil; turn halfway through the cooking time and spritz with oil again.	Coat with Blackened Seasoning (page 17).
French fries, thick	3 large potatoes	15 to 20 min	380°F	Spritz the basket with oil; toss fries in 1 tablespoon oil, season with salt and pepper; shake halfway through the cooking time and spritz with oil.	Coat with Creole Seasoning (page 16).
French fries, thin	3 large potatoes	14 to 16 min	380°F	Spritz the basket with oil; toss fries in 1 tablespoon oil, season with salt and pepper; shake halfway through the cooking time and spritz with oil.	Coat with Creole Seasoning (page 16).
Hamburgers	4 (4-ounce) patties	8 to 12 min	400°F	Spritz air fryer basket with oil; turn burgers halfway through the cooking time.	Mix in 1 tablespoon Cajun Seasoning (page 16) per pound of hamburger.
Potatoes, baked	2 or 3 large potatoes	40 min	400°F	Cut 5 slits in each potato and brush with oil.	Serve with Bacon-Wrapped Pork Tenderloin (page 86).
Potatoes, wedges	1½ pounds	20 to 25 min	400°F	Toss in 2 tablespoons oil before cooking; spritz basket with oil; shake halfway through the cooking time and spritz with oil.	Toss with Creole Seasoning (page 16).
Sausage patties	1 pound	8 to 10 min	400°F	Turn halfway through the cooking time.	Serve with Drop Biscuits (page 24).
Squash	1 pound	12 min	400°F	Spritz the basket with oil; shake halfway through the cooking time and spritz again with oil.	Coat slices in All-Purpose Breading (page 18).
Sweet potatoes, whole	2 or 3	35 to 40 min	380°F	Cut 5 slits in each sweet potato and brush with oil.	Serve with honey butter.

FROZEN FOODS

Frozen Food	Quantity	Time	Temp	Tips	Spice It Up
Bread dough	1 loaf	15 to 20 min	350°F	Thaw and proof the bread dough as directed on the package; spritz the pan with oil before baking.	Brush the top with butter and sprinkle with 1 teaspoon Creole Seasoning (page 16) before baking.
Breaded chicken breasts	2 breasts	20 to 22 min	375°F	Turn halfway through the cooking time.	Serve with Hot Honey Mustard Dip (page 19).
Breaded chicken tenders	1 (25-ounce) bag	12 min	390°F	For extra-crispy tenders, spritz with oil before cooking.	Serve with Hot Honey Mustard Dip (page 19).
Breaded fish fillets	5 fillets	10 min	375°F	Shake the basket after 5 minutes.	Serve with Pecan Tartar Sauce (page 21).
Breaded shrimp	1 pound	9 min	400°F	Shake the basket halfway through the cooking time.	Serve with Pecan Tartar Sauce (page 21).
Chicken breasts	2 chicken breasts	20 to 22 min	375°F	Spritz basket with oil; flip chicken halfway through the cooking time.	Coat with Blackened Seasoning (page 17) before cooking.
Chicken nuggets	1 (12-ounce) package	10 min	400°F	Flip halfway through the cooking time.	Serve with Hot Honey Mustard Dip (page 19).
Chicken wings	12 wings	12 to 15 min	360°F	Shake the basket halfway through the cooking time.	Coat with Creole Seasoning (page 16) before cooking.
Corn dogs	6 corn dogs	8 to 10 min	390°F	Shake the basket or flip the corn dogs halfway through the cooking time.	Serve with Hot Honey Mustard Dip (page 19).
Fish fillets	10 ounces	14 min	400°F	Spritz basket with oil; flip fish halfway through the cooking time.	Coat with Cajun Seasoning before cooking (page 16).
French fries (thick cut)	1 pound	18 min	400°F	Spritz the basket with oil; shake halfway through the cooking time.	Serve with Garlic Chicken Wings (page 79).

Frozen Food	Quantity	Time	Temp	Tips	Spice It Up
French fries (thin cut)	1¼ pounds	14 min	400°F	Spritz the basket with oil; shake halfway through the cooking time.	Serve with Garlic Chicken Wings (page 79).
Hash browns	1 pound, or 6 individual hash brown patties	15 min	370°F	Flip once during cooking to ensure even crispiness.	Sprinkle the top with 1 tablespoon Cajun Seasoning (page 16) before cooking.
Meatballs	1 pound	10 to 11 min	350°F	Flip halfway through the cooking time.	Serve with Peachy Barbecue Sauce (page 20).
Mozzarella sticks	1 (11-ounce) package	8 min	400°F	Optional: Spritz mozzarella sticks with oil before cooking for an even, crisp exterior.	Serve with the dipping sauce for Fried Green Tomatoes (page 38).
Onion rings	1 (12-ounce) package	8 min	400°F	Spritz air fryer with oil before frying. Flip onion rings halfway through the cooking time.	Serve with the dipping sauce for Fried Green Tomatoes (page 38).
Pizza rolls	10 pizza rolls	5 to 7 min	375°F	Spritz air fryer with oil before frying. Flip pizza rolls halfway through the cooking time.	Serve with the dipping sauce for Fried Green Tomatoes (page 38).
Sweet potato fries	1 pound	15 to 17 min	400°F	Spritz basket with oil before frying. Shake halfway through the cooking time.	Toss with 1 tablespoon Cajun Seasoning (page 16) before cooking.
Tater tots	12 to 16 ounces	8 to 10 min	400°F	Spritz air fryer with oil before frying. Place tots in a single layer with no overlap. Shake the basket halfway through the cooking time.	Serve with Crispy Dill Chicken Strips (page 75).
Veggie burger	4 patties	8 to 10 min	350°F	Space burgers in a single layer with no touching or overlap. Flip once.	Serve with Hot Honey Mustard Dip (page 19).

MEASUREMENT CONVERSIONS

Volume Equivalents (Liquid)

US Standard	US Standard (ounces)	Metric (approximate)
2 tablespoons	1 fl. oz.	30 mL
¼ cup	2 fl. oz.	60 mL
½ cup	4 fl. oz.	120 mL
1 cup	8 fl. oz.	240 mL
1½ cups	12 fl. oz.	355 mL
2 cups or 1 pint	16 fl. oz.	475 mL
4 cups or 1 quart	32 fl. oz.	1 L
1 gallon	128 fl. oz.	4 L

Oven Temperatures

Fahrenheit (F)	Celsius (C) (approximate)
250°F	120°C
300°F	150°C
325°F	165°C
350°F	180°C
375°F	190°C
400°F	200°C
425°F	220°C
450°F	230°C

Volume Equivalents (Dry)

US Standard	Metric (approximate)
⅛ teaspoon	0.5 mL
¼ teaspoon	1 mL
½ teaspoon	2 mL
¾ teaspoon	4 mL
1 teaspoon	5 mL
1 tablespoon	15 mL
¼ cup	59 mL
⅓ cup	79 mL
½ cup	118 mL
⅔ cup	156 mL
¾ cup	177 mL
1 cup	235 mL
2 cups or 1 pint	475 mL
3 cups	700 mL
4 cups or 1 quart	1 L

Weight Equivalents

US Standard	Metric (approximate)
½ ounce	15 g
1 ounce	30 g
2 ounces	60 g
4 ounces	115 g
8 ounces	225 g
12 ounces	340 g
16 ounces or 1 pound	455 g

RECIPE NOTES

INDEX

ACKNOWLEDGMENTS

We would like to thank our publisher, Rockridge Press/Callisto Media, for making our dream a reality—twice. Thanks to the editorial staff—Elizabeth Castoria, for thinking of us as the "resident Southern queens"; Lauren Ladoceour, for her encouragement and guidance; and to all of the production team. Also, thanks to Mike Deweese for the lovely author photos. It really does take a village to create a book.

Pam would like to thank the following: my husband, Bryan, who patiently tried all the recipes—no matter how many times we remade them—and took me out to dinner when I was tired of cooking; my son, Ashton, who didn't complain *too much* when I listened to my "cooking playlist" and didn't get upset when I accidentally fed him an ingredient he was allergic to; my son-in-law, Justin, my mother-in-law, Mary Frances, and my neighbor, Mary Veazey, for taste testing our recipes; and all my friends, family, and readers who encouraged me, either in person or through comments, emails, and messages.

Brittany would like to thank the following: This book could not have existed without the help and infinite patience of my family and friends. I'd first like to extend my gratitude to my husband, my brother, and my dad for sampling all the recipes before they ever made it into the cookbook. Secondly, I'd like to thank Taylor Shook and Alex Pilgrim for trying all the things I made in middle school, when I didn't know how to cook. Finally, I'd especially like to acknowledge Lindzie Strickland and Abigail Agostino for starting Cookbook Club and diving into the hardest cookbook for our first meeting—it was the crash course to cooking confidence I didn't know I needed.

ABOUT THE AUTHORS

Pam Wattenbarger and **Brittany Wattenbarger**
are a mother-and-daughter team and native Southerners. They've
been influenced by homestyle cooking all their lives and write about
traditional Southern dishes with allergy-friendly adaptations on their
website, SimplySouthernMom.com.

CPSIA information can be obtained
at www.ICGtesting.com
Printed in the USA
BVHW021655020720
582864BV00009B/130